Praise for
The Next Little Black Book of Success

"*The Next Little Black Book of Success* is exactly what we need in this moment: equal parts wisdom, courage, and care. Elaine, Marsha, and Rhonda don't just tell us how to succeed; they show us how to lead with intention, resilience, and generosity in a world that too often overlooks our brilliance. This book is a roadmap, a mirror, and a reminder that none of us rises alone."

—Daisy Auger-Domínguez, author of
Burnt Out to Lit Up and *Inclusion Revolution*

"An outstanding update to an essential career guidebook. It provides key advice on how to successfully navigate the new realities of the workplace."

—Henry McGee, senior lecturer of
business administration at Harvard Business School

"A brilliant guide that reminds us that leadership is not only about personal success but also about legacy—and lifting others up as we rise. It's about shaping a future where every seat at the table is earned and shared. These principles have been central to my own career journey and success."

—Maria Weaver, managing director of Oaklins DeSilva+Phillips
and former global president of Warner Music Experience

"Elaine, Marsha, and Rhonda offer invaluable lessons on leading with confidence, authenticity, and purpose. This book will inspire you to rise higher and bring others along."

—David Harper, managing principal of The Advisory Alliance

"Reading this book is like opening a precious treasure box. In it, the authors share truths for discerning your personal goals; what it takes to be yourself inside and outside of the "system"; and how to pay it forward, all shared from a place of deep caring. At a time when many leaders are feeling the stress of uncertainty, let this book be your guide. If you incorporate half of the wisdom found within, you will be far ahead of the game!"

—Jane Hyun, global leadership strategist, author of *Leadership Toolkit for Asians* and *Breaking the Bamboo Ceiling,* and co-author of *Flex*

"*The Next Little Black Book of Success* is a tremendously engaging and relevant guide for moving through the professional world. But it is also a genuine treasure house of enduring, powerful, and practical leadership lessons that are invaluable for navigating life in these challenging times."

—Rev. Dr. Derrick Harkins, dean of Graduate and Leadership Studies at Virginia Union University

"Indeed, the band is back together with a fresh yet profound message to women on the rise. Sage wisdom and actionable insights leap from the pages."

—Amy Kemp, author of *It's All About the Dough* and program associate for the National Association for Multi-Ethnicity in Communications (NAMIC).

"If you are ready to take the next steps on your career journey, *The Next Little Black Book of Success: New Laws of Leadership for Black Women* is a must-read. It's an insightful guide to help you identify and achieve your goals, focus your energy, and harness your power."

—Ruth Hassell-Thompson, former New York State Senator

"The wisdom in these pages is both timely and timeless. Elaine, Marsha, and Rhonda have once again given Black women leaders the tools we need to rise with clarity and confidence. *The Next Little Black Book of Success* is a must-read, equipping us to lead with power and purpose as the game—and its rules—continue to shift in real time."

—Valerie Irick Rainford, founder and CEO of Elloree Talent Strategies

THE

NEXT

LITTLE

BLACK

BOOK

OF

SUCCESS

ELAINE MERYL BROWN,

MARSHA HAYGOOD,

AND RHONDA JOY MCLEAN

THE
NEXT
LITTLE
BLACK
BOOK
OF
SUCCESS

NEW LAWS OF LEADERSHIP
FOR BLACK WOMEN

STOREHOUSE VOICES

NEW YORK

STOREHOUSE VOICES
An imprint of the Crown Publishing Group
A division of Penguin Random House LLC
1745 Broadway
New York, NY 10019
storehousevoices.com
penguinrandomhouse.com

STOREHOUSE VOICES and the Storehouse Voices colophon are trademarks of Penguin Random House LLC.

Library of Congress Cataloging-in-Publication Data has been applied for.

Hardcover ISBN 978-0-593-72948-9
Ebook ISBN 978-0-593-72949-6

Editor and Associate publisher: Porscha Burke
Production editor: Isabella Franco
Text designer: Andrea Lau
Production: Jessica Heim
Copy editor: Mimi Lipson
Proofreaders: Hope Clarke, Vicki Fischer, and Eldes Tran
Publisher: Tamira Chapman
Editorial director: Jennifer Baker
Publishing associate: Isabela Alcantara

Manufactured in the United States of America

1st Printing

First Edition

The authorized representative in the EU for product safety and compliance is Penguin Random House Ireland, Morrison Chambers, 32 Nassau Street, Dublin D02 YH68, Ireland, https://eu-contact.penguin.ie.

*Lifting up all Black women in leadership and in life.
Let's continue to help one another win!*

CONTENTS

1 **The First Person You Lead Is Yourself** 1

*High self-confidence is a cornerstone of success and affects how others
perceive you. Know your value and self-worth, and always put your
best foot forward.*

2 **Acknowledge That There Is a Game and Accept That
You Must Play** 6

*Don't ignore office politics that may shift and office culture that will
likely remain. Assess your work environment; listen to and understand
what is being said versus what is not being said. Know that you are
not entitled to success and need to understand the game in order to
play.*

3 **Rise Above the Racism** 9

*Even the best managers can succumb to unconscious biases or implicit
prejudice and favoritism based on what is most comfortable and
familiar to them.*

FOREWORD

Before our first book was published, we came together with a group of Black women corporate executives who met for dinner regularly to have fun and share ideas, experiences, and stories. We helped one another with challenges and celebrated our leadership successes. After years of supporting one another privately, we thought it was important to share our stories of leadership with others, including those in the next generation. We could not find any books relevant to Black women in the leadership space, which only confirmed that we needed to get our messages out there so what we learned wouldn't get lost. We decided to write the book we wished we'd had in the beginning of our careers.

But why another book on leadership from us, and why now?

These are fair questions that we have posed to ourselves. We have concluded that since our first book, the leadership landscape and the way we work have significantly changed. We thought it was important to share updates and our insights with you.

While we believe that the fundamental principles of leadership that we outlined in our first book and made interactive in our second (the workbook) have essentially remained the same, the way we lead and navigate the workplace has changed dramatically. With rapid advances in technology and artificial intelligence, the ongoing onslaught of environmental uncertainties, worldwide health pandemics, and sociopolitical challenges facing human and civil rights, leaders, and their teams have had to pivot and re-strategize to adjust to these changing times.

As Black women, we already know we have more hurdles to overcome than others. However, leadership responsibilities have shifted quickly from managing employees in person and on-site to routinely running teams of people who may be working partly or fully remotely, who may live in different time zones, countries, and/or cultures and speak other languages. Leaders are being called upon to keep their team members productive and upbeat, despite the extraordinary toll of fluctuating economies and disruptive political realities. It's important now, more than ever, for good leaders to find new ways to motivate themselves and others.

Working in hybrid office situations has, to say the least, changed our approach to business. Without having regular in-person access to individuals, we must be creative with our communication styles in order to ensure that all participants in our workplaces are seen as well as heard. Wearing multiple hats requires that we must have various skill sets to successfully lead today's workforces.

Since our first book, many of you have told us that you've been transformed, enlightened, and guided by our advice and still turn to our books as sources of reference. Women—and men—from various ethnicities and cultures have told us they have benefited from reading about our experiences and practicing our strategies.

As times have changed, we have changed as well. We have expanded a successful, preexisting business and started a new one; coached leaders at every level; become board members; transitioned into new careers; obtained degrees in higher education; and mentored others, from young people to seasoned executives. With all that we continue to experience, we wanted to combine our collective knowledge again and share it with you here.

In this third book, we address new hurdles in the leadership arena and propose strategies for overcoming them, while expanding our thinking on new topics and updating those already discussed. Our work with leaders and individuals at every level over the years has inspired us to craft clear, concise, and practical steps for developing and improving our leadership skills and styles.

While our first book has been described as being like a mentor in your pocket and our workbook as a call to action, this book is your map to the future, so that you can become the best leader you can be and help foster the next generation of leaders.

We hope you get just as much out of this book as you did from our first two.

ELAINE'S STORY

My running joke is that our first book on leadership has been so well-received and popular that it now feels like it is leading us. To some extent it is. It has been an honor and a blessing to share our new experiences and observations about the ways we work and live our lives in this new book. Like many of us, I've had to pivot, but I've also had to focus on what's next at this stage of my career and how to continue to lead myself. Since I now have the freedom and flexibility to create my own structure, I took the leap to pursue my passion as a full-time writer and learn more about my craft. I followed my own advice, upskilled and now have an MFA in Creative Writing from Reinhardt University, and am currently working on my third novel. Most importantly, writing this new book has reunited me with Marsha and Rhonda; it's like getting the band back together, and together our passion is to help you tap into your leadership potential, provide you with concrete steps to soar, claim your seat at the table if that is what you want, or create your own table and sit at the head of it. Whatever your leadership goals, I hope you will be inspired by our book and that it will be transformative. Over the years, Marsha, Rhonda, and I have poured into each other, and now we are grateful to have the opportunity to pour into you.

MARSHA'S STORY

I was blessed with a mother who drilled into me the belief that I could do anything I set my mind and energy toward, and I believed her. Although my mom never worked in a large corporation, she was well-read and a good listener, and she always seemed to teach, motivate, and lift the confidence of those she came in contact with.

What this taught me was to show up with a sense of confidence and a can-do attitude even at a very young age. That doesn't mean that I didn't have missteps along the way, but my attitude was and continues to be to not think of them as failures but learning experiences.

- As I have grown from receptionist to successful entrepreneur, I have shared what I have learned with others. Look for opportunities to learn from those you admire.
- Listen to what is said as well as what is meant.
- Learn to show up, speak up, and ask for what you want in order to get what you need.
- Align your attitude, behavior, and values with your ambition.

With these guidelines in mind, I have been able to turn adversity into triumph and reach back and bring others along with me.

For many years while working in the corporate arena, I experienced some difficult and unfair situations. However, there are two very important lessons that have served me well: (1) Reflect on your "WHY." What do you want to get from the situation? Trust me, it is usually more than $$$. And (2) use strategy versus emotion to get what you need. This takes practice, but believe me, strategy keeps you in control of a situation while emotion puts you in a vulnerable state and allows negative thoughts and behaviors to surface.

I hope that this book, along with our first *Little Black Book of Success* and the companion workbook, will serve as a reference and motivator for you to continue to **move forward with purpose.**

RHONDA'S STORY

My journey—from integrating into my small-town high school with my teenage friends during the early years of the Civil Rights Movement to earning four degrees and working as an attorney and executive for four decades in the public, private, and academic sectors—has been interesting, enlightening, challenging, and rewarding. In recent years, I have enjoyed sharing what I have learned with students and clients, including strategies for pivoting as leaders when unforeseen shifts in our lives and careers test our capabilities. My experiences have shown that leadership opportunities are not limited by age, titles, or timelines, and what may seem like setbacks can be launchpads for even greater success. I hope the practical strategies we have outlined here will embolden you to move beyond your fears—especially in uncertain times—and become the leaders you are destined to be and that our world needs.

TOOLS TO CHART YOUR
ROAD MAP TO SUCCESS

In our first book, *The Little Black Book of Success,* we strongly recommended you create a Personal Leadership Notebook (PLN) to jot down your insights and ideas while reading through the chapters. We suggested you use your PLN to keep track of your accomplishments, progress, and goals. Then we wrote *The Little Black Book of Success Workbook,* which we refer to as your personal-call-to-action plan. It follows our first book chapter-by-chapter with exercises to help you take a deeper dive into your leadership skills and give you an understanding of your strengths and areas that may need improvement. While you can certainly benefit from using this workbook on its own, we recommend working with both books to achieve maximum benefit.

We also strongly recommend you create a PLN while reading this book. Your PLN can also be a place where you keep contact information, important dates, project results, or any other data relevant to your leadership journey. Be sure your PLN can fit into your purse, handbag, backpack, or briefcase since you want to always have it handy. Your PLN should grow along with your leadership journey, so don't be surprised if you have volumes of material. It also doesn't matter what your PLN looks like—an old diary that you never wrote in, a plain spiral notebook with folders to keep track of your notes, or a brand-new fancy and colorful journal.

Together, *The Little Black Book of Success,* the workbook, and *The Next Little Black Book of Success* are a trilogy—dynamic resources to advance you in your leadership journey and move you forward on your career trajectory to create a powerful legacy for you, your family, your community, and others on this path for generations to come.

THE
NEXT
LITTLE
BLACK
BOOK
OF
SUCCESS

The First Person You Lead Is Yourself

High self-confidence is a cornerstone of success
and affects how others perceive you. Know your value and
self-worth, and always put your best foot forward.

As an integral part of the American and global workforce, Black women hold roles at every level and within all industries. It is important and necessary that we bring the skills, will, and leadership presence, no matter what position we hold—whether janitor, chief of staff, or chief operating officer. While there should be no denying the value we bring to the organizations and situations we engage in, we must remember to carry ourselves as VIPs.

You are a very important person—even if you have never held a leadership position or were told you did not have leadership potential as you were growing up. It starts with you being the best you, unapologetically!

We already know that having high self-esteem, a positive attitude, and executive presence are important in any role—in the office or in our personal lives. High self-esteem is critical in leadership, period. Women with high self-esteem have the inner strength to overcome mistakes, confront adversity, and meet their leadership goals. Self-acceptance and positive self-talk can cultivate a confident attitude and attract the attention of others, including those who may be sponsors. A sponsor is usually a senior person who has power and influence and is willing to use their influence to give you visibility for new and higher-level assignments. They speak

highly of you to other decision-makers and are willing to stake their reputation on your success based on your performance in various situations,
your character, and your reliability, attitude, and readiness. They sing
your praises when you're not in the room. Often, you don't even know
who your sponsor is. It is therefore important to speak up, show up, and
let people see you in the best light possible to demonstrate that you are
sponsor-worthy.

The way you feel about yourself—the way you feel inside—is going to
impact how you perform on your job and your ability to lead *you*. After
all, you have to lead yourself before you can lead others.

There is also a connection between self-confidence and leadership.
Self-confidence is at the core of leadership. In fact, it's the very foundation of leadership. Working from a confident self-image is like building
a house on concrete that can withstand all the elements and storms bat-
tering against it, as opposed to building a house on shaky ground—one
that is sure to collapse. Someone who lacks confidence is afraid to take
risks, try new things, take on new assignments, meet new people, and
put themselves in new situations. A leader with self-confidence thinks
positively about the future, is willing to take risks, and will step outside
her comfort zone to achieve her personal and professional goals. If you
don't have the self-confidence to lead, gaining followers will be difficult
or next to impossible.

However, in the world and in the workplace, external factors may try
to undermine your self-confidence and lower your self-esteem. Troubling
broadcast news media, headlines about global events, negative social
media posts, unkind comments by an ex from a personal relationship
gone sour are all examples of how our minds can be bombarded with
negative images. The workplace is another.

You will have to refuse to give in to negative images and negative
thinking that can hold you back. One of our readers shared a story with
us, from her early days after getting a promotion. She overheard her supervisor asking someone, "Do you think she's really capable? This is a big

job." While, instinctively, she wanted to shrink back—if the boss didn't think she was capable, how could she?—she knew putting that negative thought into her head wouldn't position her for success. She fashioned a reply to his question in her own mind. *I know I am capable of doing this job. I wouldn't have the opportunity to be considered otherwise. Not only have I worked hard to develop the skills for this role, I have also studied this business and served its most successful players for a very long time. I am capable, qualified, and positioned to succeed.* She continued to repeat this last line over and over, turning any negative thought into a positive one.

It's imperative to have a positive mental attitude and change your mindset with positive self-talk, even though the negative forces in the workplace are real. You must stay focused on your true self, your God-given talents, both your hard and your soft skills, and become a savvy player in the work game. Once you are in the game of work, you have committed yourself to play.

Understand that some supervisors may not feel comfortable giving you honest feedback—that might not be their style, or they may be concerned about their comments being misconstrued as biased. Unconscious biases are implicit judgments based on stereotypes (often rooted in race, gender, and ability without conscious awareness).

According to the "State of Black Women in Corporate America" report, women of color, and Black women in particular, tend to receive less support and encouragement from their managers.* They are less likely to have managers showcase their work, advocate for them to take on new roles and responsibilities, or give them opportunities to manage people and projects. Black women are also less likely to report that their manager helps them navigate organizational politics or balance work and personal life. The report also states that Black women are much less likely than their non-Black colleagues to interact with senior leaders at

---

* Lean In and McKinsey & Company, The State of the Black Woman in Corporate America, 2020.

work, which means they have fewer opportunities to get noticed and, therefore, they have fewer opportunities for sponsorship within their organizations.

Microaggressions can demean, disrespect, or be dismissive and are a common experience for Black women at work. Worst-case scenario, an accumulation of microaggressions over time could even contribute to what is known as *imposter syndrome*, where one doubts their own accomplishments and ability to do their job, especially in comparison to their colleagues' skills and achievements. Too often, brilliant women of color sabotage themselves—sometimes without even knowing that they are doing it—so that they never become the leaders they are capable of being or achieve the level of leadership success they deserve.

The first step to handling any sense of unfairness in the business environment is to accept that prejudice of all kinds exists. Indeed, many of us are prejudiced, and instead of letting these feelings get in your way, you must find creative ways to move around them. You may be frustrated; at times, you may want to give up and leave your position altogether. But you know the old adage: wherever you go, there you are. And the same issues are going to present themselves time after time, so you may as well work on navigating the system with self-esteem, self-confidence, a positive attitude, and strategies to keep you going forward and focusing on your leadership goals. Your leadership journey is very important, and you're in it for the duration. It's not a race, but it does require a steady commitment to progress.

It's no longer a secret: leaders are not just born, leaders are made. The truth is, even the ones who are born have a lot to learn. From the top down, from the most senior to the most entry-level positions, it's imperative to stay strategic and intentional along your leadership journey. Leaders who have high self-esteem and a positive self-image value themselves and turn self-doubt into confidence. Remain motivated and believe in yourself. Be prepared to win and suffer losses along the way, but always hold your head up high. Remember that you are a VIP and already successful or on your way to success. Surround yourself with people who will lift you up and propel you to move forward. The first person you lead is yourself.

....

"You are a baaaad mamma jamma!"

"You have to lead yourself before you can lead others."

SHOUT-OUT

"If they don't give you a seat at the table, bring a folding chair."

—Shirley Chisholm

2

Acknowledge That There Is a Game and Accept That You Must Play

Don't ignore office politics that may shift and office culture that will likely remain. Assess your work environment; listen to and understand what is being said versus what is not being said. Know that you are not entitled to success and need to understand the game in order to play.

To be more successful, you must not only do your job well, but you must be aware of the unwritten rules of navigating your work environment. This is what is referred to as "the game," and the game played at work is known as *organizational norms,* also known as *company culture* and *office politics.*

You may not want to play the game, but it is important that you observe, listen, and learn these unwritten rules within the organization in order to be recognized for opportunities or advancement. Your survival or success may depend on it.

Before joining an organization, learn as much as possible about its mission, values, and vision. If the values, vision, and standards of behavior do not align with yours, you should look elsewhere!

Once you join the organization, you should pay attention to the power structure within the company, identify who has decision-making authority, and familiarize yourself with the chain of command. Note that titles may or may not determine who has power and how information flows and decisions are made.

Understanding these dynamics and unwritten procedures can help you get things done. Look for opportunities to listen to what is being said and by whom.

Build Positive Relationships

* Networking and attending meetings and events you are invited to are good ways to gain visibility—and to observe communication styles, noting how personal and professional information flows.
* Be personable, but *listen* more than you share your information. Remember that these learning opportunities can help you seek and gain support from others when needed.
* Foster relationships with colleagues across different departments, because a strong network can provide support as well as formal and informal information.
* If you are unsure about certain aspects of the company culture or the office politics, seek guidance from an experienced and trusted colleague or mentor; however, you may want to remain neutral and curious. Ask, don't tell.
* Social media is also a great way to learn about those you meet and interact with. Note that you should be mindful of your own online presence, as your professional image extends beyond the office.

Every workplace is different, and the game may be played at one organization very differently than it is at another organization. Being an active learner is imperative to your success. Maintaining a positive attitude, being adaptable to various work styles, and being careful about what you share and with whom can help you navigate and advance your career.

While it is important to learn how to "play the game," authenticity is also key. Being genuine about your values will make your work experiences more positive and less stressful and will help you as you move forward on your leadership journey.

....

"Just when you think you've mastered the game,
the goal posts will be moved."

"Not playing the game can put you on the sidelines."

SHOUT-OUT

"A lot of people notice when you succeed,
but they don't see what it takes to get there."

—Dawn Staley

3

Rise Above the Racism

Even the best managers can succumb to unconscious biases or
implicit prejudice and favoritism based on
what is most comfortable and familiar to them.

Systemic racism continues to exist, and in some places, it is still on the rise. Black and brown people in our criminal justice system are still incarcerated at higher rates than others. In education, Black and brown communities continue to receive less funding and resources. Black women have higher mortality rates than other women. We are more likely to face employment discrimination. The wealth gap persists, limiting our ability to get ahead; and let's not forget voter suppression: practices put in place that make it difficult for us to vote.

Every day we must guard our emotions and decide if we are going to let our circumstances affect our joy and happiness.

Don't let racism that exists in the workplace discourage you. It's important to shield yourself against these behaviors. Starting your day with a gratitude routine is one way to set yourself up for success. Developing a resilient mentality can help you bounce back and transform difficult experiences into the fuel that propels your future. You are worth it!

We cannot let the pressures of the world, or other people's issues or prejudices, keep us from all the good things that life has in store. In other words, don't let racism steal your joy! A positive mindset ultimately yields positive results.

Understand that this does not mean you should not speak up or call out those who are disrespectful or uncivil. However, it does mean that you will not let racism, microaggressions, or disrespectful actions get in the way of you reaching your goals. It is important to be aware of your personal pressure points (also known as *triggers*), and plan beforehand how best to manage your responses when your buttons are pushed, because over time you will surely be tested.

Practice using strategy over emotion as you pursue your quest to gain the knowledge and experience that are needed to advance your leadership journey. For example, if someone says something that is racially offensive, rather than trying to argue the point, ask them, "What makes you say that?" or "Can you give me an example?" Get them to think, and come up with answers that address their racist comments. There is no reason for you to get upset over their ignorance.

Know that we all have experiences of being overlooked, invisible, and unfairly treated at some point in our lives, but this should not cause us to give up and lose faith in ourselves and our abilities to move forward for personal and professional growth. There always have been and always will be people who will try to push back on your efforts to expand equity and opportunities.

This is when you recite your affirmations, embrace your resilience and self-confidence, and lean on your circle of positive supporters. Build your *success team*, or *personal board of directors*—people whom you respect and trust—so that you can support and lift one another up during these difficult times. Think about who you know, who you need to know, and who needs to know you. To keep it active, stay in touch with these individuals using text, Zoom, and email to check in—even if it's to say, "Just thinking about you."

The individuals on your success team do not have to look like you. The more diverse your success team is, the more perspectives you will get so you can draw your own conclusions and decide how best to handle different or difficult situations. Know that you cannot please everyone, and you cannot "fix stupid" or change racist attitudes. However, you may be able to enlighten others or have opportunities for teachable moments by actively challenging and questioning stereotypes when they are encountered.

Most importantly, what you can do is be the best version of yourself. Be the best person you can be using your knowledge and skills with integrity. In other words, stand up for your values.

Remember: You are worthy of all you want to accomplish, so don't let racism, microaggressions, and unfair treatment dim your sparkle. If your light is too bright for some, get them some sunglasses and move on.

....

"Don't let racism steal your joy and
determination for leadership success."

SHOUT-OUTS

"You are the light. Never let anyone—any person or any force—
dampen, dim, or diminish your light."

—John Lewis

....

"Turn your wounds into wisdom."

—Oprah Winfrey

4

Microaggressions — What You Need to Know About Conscious and Unconscious Biases

If your manager hasn't been exposed to people who look like you, here's what you need to know about conscious and unconscious biases.

Microaggressions are subtle verbal or nonverbal insults or behaviors that send negative messages. They can be disguised as compliments and are usually said or done to demonstrate a sense of superiority. They may be unconscious or unintentional, but they are not void of racism or discrimination. These comments or actions may include insults regarding race, gender, religious beliefs, special abilities, sexual preferences, or lifestyles. A few examples of statements include:

- You are so articulate!
- Did you really write this?
- How do you think Black people would respond to that situation?
- Is that your real hair?
- You don't look gay.

Even in hybrid workplaces, you may be impacted by passive-aggressive behaviors of managers, colleagues, clients, or others you come in contact with. Despite the progress we have made in the work world as Black women, we may still have to deal with inconsistent and insulting conduct from others. Whether you are entry-level, middle management, or a senior executive, you have probably already experienced one or more microaggressions. A few examples of circumstances you may have encountered include:

- Although you have called a business meeting and are responsible for it, someone other than you (whether junior or senior to you) assumes control of or attempts to run your meeting and does not identify or recognize you or your position.
- Although you have "raised your hand" in an online meeting where input was specifically requested, you are never given an opportunity to share your ideas, and your suggestions in the chat room or Q & A portal are not acknowledged or addressed.
- Despite your designation as a manager, senior executives, peers, or others routinely reach beyond you to address your direct reports and give them assignments without consulting you.

Experiencing these behaviors can be disconcerting and unsettling, and addressing them can be awkward and prickly, but here are a few steps you can take:

1. Know your value and stand your ground.
   You must know your worth as a person and a professional and what you bring to any table. Be brave, strategic, and clear in your communications.
2. Determine whether the slight or conduct needs to be addressed.
   Could you have misunderstood or overreacted? You may want to ask the

person to explain their comment or action. If you can safely do so, vet your perception of the conduct with someone that you trust. Sometimes the best response is no response.

3. Breathe deeply and step away for a moment.

   If you are overly emotional, you may act defensively or inappropriately and hurt your standing in your organization.

4. Be sure to use your resources to consider all your options.

   Consult your knowledgeable, trusted peers, mentors, coaches, friends, or others to help strategically guide you in your deliberations.

5. If you decide to take action, speak or meet with the protagonist and make sure you are focused and clear.

   Be specific in your language and give examples of the offending conduct:

   - "I'm not sure what you mean by that. Please explain."
   - "You may not be aware of this, but you sidelined me in my meeting, and I was offended."
   - "When you reached past me to [employee name] and gave her an assignment without consulting me, that could lead to confusion and it seemed to undermine my position."

6. Outline acceptable conduct.

   "Going forward, I will be glad to work with you if you need input or action from my team." "I suggest we meet directly to discuss my ideas for ensuring the success of our projects, business divisions, etc."

If your concerns are not addressed or acknowledged, you may decide to file a formal complaint within your organization, using the protocols and processes available to you. You might also consider researching another position within or outside of your organization. Note that changing positions or organizations does not necessarily guarantee a culture change.

Whatever you decide to do, *do not lose faith in yourself!*

Microaggressions, gaslighting, and the limited beliefs of others about our capabilities are often all at play simultaneously in our evolving workplaces. Nevertheless, our faith, confidence, skills, resilience, support networks, and our will must continue to move us forward.

....

"Microaggressions are behaviors that should be addressed because they may be based on misinformation."

SHOUT-OUTS

"Ain't gonna let nobody turn me 'round."

—Negro spiritual

....

"Racism is taught in our society. . . . It is not automatic. It is learned behavior toward persons with dissimilar physical characteristics."

—attributed to Alex Haley

5

Don't Be the Workplace Mammy

Whether working in person, remotely, or in hybrid settings, women may be expected to take on the role of caregiver, or even opt in to this role subconsciously. *Resist assuming this role!* Instead, demonstrate your skills and substantive contributions.

Alongside the great strides women have made in the workplace—becoming entrepreneurs, CEOs, presidents, partners, managing directors, and beyond—we are also seeing attempts to push women back into the role of workplace "mammy": the one who supports and nurtures everyone else at the expense of her own well-being; the one whose work may not get done during normal working hours because she is so attentive to the needs and wants of others; the one doing or redoing someone else's work instead of dutifully managing her workers. While we treasure the compassion, warmth, and emotional intelligence that can make women such phenomenal leaders, those same traits may trap women in roles they have not consciously chosen.

Workplace confidante. Workplace psychologist. Workplace events planner and decorator. Workplace cook/chef. Each of these roles has its own appeal—serving in the workplace, especially in capacities in which we may be naturally skilled or well practiced, can feel rewarding, especially when it appeals to our human needs for connection and relationship. Historically, women, especially women of color / Black women, were considered to be valuable only for their caregiving skills and childbearing capabilities. This designation of women as "chief nurturers" is still deeply embedded in our society.

Does this mean you shouldn't bake the cookies or bring in the macaroni and cheese to the staff luncheon? No, certainly not! What we mean is baking the cookies or planning the workplace outing / virtual entertainment event should not be the *only* thing you are known for or the first thing people think of when they think of you.

Our contemporary office spaces may bring us into contact with colleagues, peers, and managers across the globe, from different countries, time zones, and cultures—each with their own expectations of managers and team members. When reaching across boundaries to extend the hand of friendship and get to know your fellow global workers, it is important to establish yourself as a colleague, peer, or manager—not a gofer, only there to pick up the slack or grab the coffees before a meeting begins. Even virtually, you can be tucked into the role of notetaker or nanny, such that you are expected to take care of the team but not to lead it. No matter your position, you must resist. While it may be to your advantage to be the notetaker early in your career so that you can learn how the organization functions, you may not want to continue in this role as you advance in your career. Consider using technology to assist with administrative tasks.

There is a fine line between caring *about* and caring *for* others. Trust that you can navigate this distinction as you set clear goals for yourself to learn, grow, and advance, and to help others do the same. Just be sure to take very good care of yourself before you set out to help others. Remember, you cannot pour tea out of an empty cup!

Some Black women leaders may take on too much because they feel guilty or insecure about their advancement and feel they have to "earn" their new, higher posts or positions. *No!* You have already paid for these new opportunities. You have already earned them. You deserve to be where you are.

You will respect yourself more and be respected more by others when you establish boundaries for yourself so that you can get your own more substantial work completed on time and done well. You can help others by modeling your own efficiency and effectiveness. You do not have to mother them.

Refer people to others to assist them with whatever they may need, but refrain from always providing those direct services yourself. This shift from *mothering*, or serving everyone who approaches us, to *referring* them to others may take some doing, but the transition, which is a very important one, is definitely worth it in the long run.

....

"I am not your mama!"

"You have a bigger role to play."

"Save your listening skills for understanding and
solving business problems, not other people's problems."

SHOUT-OUT

"If someone is using you, you can deny their access."

—Chante' Whisonant

Duality Is a Gift

Use your knowledge of the dominant culture and lessons learned from experiencing racism and sexism to navigate through challenging situations.

As Black women in America, we have grown up in a society where, to survive, we have to learn how to thrive in our family culture and our home community and, at the same time, in the larger society. Being the only Black person, or one of a few, in a workplace that is predominantly white is not an uncommon experience, and we should recognize that this can be an opportunity rather than a disadvantage.

Working in a corporate environment, we bring along a bicultural communication and experience that others don't have. We must use this duality to our advantage. To survive and become successful, it is not uncommon for Black people to have to be more aware of other cultures than other cultures feel they need to be aware of ours. Having grown up in two worlds puts you in a position to know more about others than they know about you.

As we learn to embrace our home training, we must hold on to principles of respect and self-respect—acknowledging cultural differences without diminishing anyone's identity or allowing anyone to diminish our own. We can and should utilize our biculturalism strategically, often allowing us to bring a varied understanding and insight to a corporate environment.

The term *code-switching* refers to the concept of double consciousness, a phrase W.E.B. Du Bois used in his classic work *The Souls of Black Folk* in 1903. He describes that double consciousness as an inward sense of "two-ness"—an internal conflict in which a subordinated or colonized group sees itself as it is and also through the eyes of its oppressors, or the dominant perspective. Black people in a racially prejudiced society had to know how to get along—they had to know what language and gestures to use—in order to survive. Flexing between those two modalities is code-switching.

From a cultural standpoint, we have learned not to communicate in the same manner all the time, in every single situation. We may use certain language to speak with family and friends that differs in tone, vocabulary, and even volume from the language we use with colleagues at work. Our body language at work may include direct eye contact, presenting an engaging face and warm, friendly smile, and behaviors that are nonthreatening. On the other hand, outside of work, we may be more relaxed, animated, free to use more pronounced gestures, to be expressive and less guarded, unconcerned about how our movements may be critiqued by others. We code switch, alternating between very different communication styles. We code switch to fit in, to put others more at ease so that it works to our advantage. This doesn't mean we're not being authentic, but rather, we're being smart and strategic about being aware of our surroundings, who we're speaking to, who our audience is, and adjusting accordingly. It means we're using our duality to our advantage.

Turn living in this world of duality and double burdens into your *superpower,* where you can navigate through issues, anticipate challenges, and share various ideas to solve problems that allow you to look at issues from both sides and offer a different perspective.

Using your duality is a leadership strategy that will also make you better prepared to deal with racism, sexism, and ageism along your personal and professional journey.

. . . .

"Being two-faced may not be such a bad thing."

"The double life of knowing your side of the tracks
while understanding the other side of the tracks
has its benefits (advantages)."

SHOUT-OUT
. . . .

"One ever feels his twoness—an American, a Negro;
two souls, two thoughts, two unreconciled strivings;
two warring ideals in one dark body, whose dogged strength
alone keeps it from being torn asunder."

—W.E.B. Du Bois

Speak Up — What You Have to Say Is Just as Important as What Others Have to Say

Your voice is your power, so speak up and make the most of it!

To be a successful leader, you must communicate clearly and share opinions and points of view in meetings. As we grow in our careers, recognizing and understanding our value and how best to utilize our strengths takes patience, practice, and confidence. One of our strengths is sharing our perspectives and our diverse ideas and experiences. Speaking up is necessary to ensure our voices are heard and our contributions are appreciated.

Clear verbal and written communications are essential to being heard, understood, and recognized. However, cultural stereotypes and fear of negative feedback often hinder our confidence in speaking up. Being one of the only women, people of color, or even being a remote worker—all this can be intimidating and sometimes prevents us from speaking up. Identifying stereotypes and biases within an organization's culture beforehand and observing, analyzing, and utilizing the communication norms in whatever setting we are in allow us to adjust as needed to get our points across.

When pushback arises, learning to use strategy rather than emotion is key. Good listening skills and asking direct follow-up questions hold people accountable and usually work better than demonstrating annoyed behaviors, being perceived as impolite, and arguing our point of view. Planning, practicing, and strategizing beforehand is a leadership strength that can and should be utilized. Pay attention and learn from others who express themselves well. Watch their body language and tone of voice—and evaluate your own and others in their presence. Note that practical exercises can enhance preparedness for speaking up and sharing ideas. Deep breathing techniques (like square breathing or four-seven-eight breathing), the recitation of positive affirmations (or writing them down and keeping them in your line of sight at work), and visualization (seeing yourself having achieved that goal or solved that issue) are just a few resources toward helping you remain empowered and confident in speaking up and presenting well.

Another technique: Take your time. Don't be afraid to suggest picking up a conversation at a later time so that you can think through the points you want and need to get across. It is more important to share your point of view. However, how you share your thoughts is even more critical.

Seeking opportunities to present and share ideas and your responses to situations can offer many benefits and can help you build support. We have all heard stories about or had experiences where our idea is ignored, and then, when someone else says the same idea, it is discussed and accepted. This can be frustrating, but one possible strategy is to publicly thank the person for agreeing with your idea and express how you might work together to move the idea forward. Resilience, strategy, mindset, and tone can help keep you in conversation and demonstrate your leadership ability.

As hard as it may be sometimes, you should keep a positive attitude and focus on what you can control and what you can accomplish. Your ideas and opinions can influence and inspire others, and by speaking up, you have the potential to drive change and make a positive impact.

Learn from these encounters so that you are prepared to avoid or control similar experiences, as they will surely happen more than once during your leadership journey. Remember, someone is always paying attention to your ideas. How you respond to various situations can lead to gaining allies, mentors, sponsors, and opportunities for career growth.

Note that speaking up also requires asking for and accepting constructive feedback. This often comes into play when discussing a desired change—in job title, reporting structure, salary, etc. If this is the case, feedback should be requested long before your formal review time so that needed adjustments can be made.

. . . .

"Your voice is your power, so use it to the fullest!"

"Understand that you can be assertive
without being aggressive: tone matters."

SHOUT-OUT
. . . .

"Courage is what it takes to stand up and speak;
courage is also what it takes to sit down and listen."

—commonly attributed to Winston Churchill

8

Be "Seen" When You Are Working Remotely

Being present in the office has advantages for in-person contact and communications, and today's workplace requires you to be creative in making your presence known and elevating your visibility when working remotely as well.

Following the sweeping transformation of office culture brought about by the COVID-19 pandemic in 2020, many of us have now had some experience working remotely—flattening our communications with co-workers from a dynamic mix of phone calls, conference room gatherings, and in-office drive-bys to two-dimensional meetings hosted on virtual platforms and overwhelmed email inboxes. Today, while many organizations are implementing return-to-office policies—formally or informally encouraging employees to work in person or in hybrid arrangements—whether you work away from the office some, most, or all of the time, you must still cultivate and maintain work relationships in order to be successful.

How can you be "seen" when you are not physically in your work venue? First and foremost, you must make sure that you are present in every way that you can be:

- Don't hide behind your name, logo, or avatar. Show your face!
- Take every opportunity offered to add an agenda item or present on an issue of importance to your team. If the opportunity is not offered, volunteer!

- Pose questions and comments through the chat or Q & A or other appropriate portals on your screen. Raise your hand, using the appropriate icon!

- If you feel you are being ignored, double check your virtual connection and then reach out to the team leader / meeting manager to offer your ideas directly. Make sure that your offerings are on point and informative, not disruptive or distracting.

- Send articles of interest to the team and post links to them, as appropriate, in the online portals available to you.

- If you do not already have one-on-one meetings established on a regular basis with your managers and/or your team members, create an opportunity to meet on- or offline whenever possible.

- For all meetings, make sure you prepare your own agenda for the discussion, which may include your ideas, accomplishments, your questions, your skill-building goals, and suggestions for moving the team forward. Not every meeting needs to be long in order to be effective.

- Take part in or help to organize informal virtual gatherings— particularly those in which you can get to know one another better and understand the skills and strengths you each bring to the table.

- Look for opportunities to collaborate with others, whether online or offline. You can demonstrate your acuity and skill in getting things done, no matter where you or your team members are located.

- Be sure to share your accomplishments with key members of your organization, especially when you do not have a chance to see your colleagues, peers, managers, direct reports, or clients regularly. Share a newsletter (a short one-pager) outlining your and your team's accomplishments and citing new ideas and progress on long-term goals, projects, or assignments. It's okay to brag and talk about achievements.

• Share what you know and invite input as appropriate so that you are viewed as a thinker, contributor, and innovator.

Black women leaders and aspiring leaders are very creative, finding ways to work authentically in the new hybrid workplace. Use your creativity to be seen and valued, no matter where you are physically located.

. . . .

"Show 'em what you got!"

"Doesn't matter if you're shy or an introvert— not being on camera is not an option."

"*Represent!* Foster a sense of community, team, brand identity, and positive self-image."

SHOUT-OUT

"Be so good they can't ignore you."

—Steve Martin

9

Who Said You Need to Have All the Answers?

Don't think that others always have all the answers or all the skills
necessary to get a particular job done or fill a particular role.
Sometimes you have to make it up or do the research as you go along.

In the post-pandemic years, when hybrid working is the norm and you may not be required to be in an office on a daily basis, it's imperative to take advantage of opportunities, now more than ever. It's true what they say: out of sight, out of mind—which is why, in this current work environment, you have to elevate your visibility so others can see your talents and leadership abilities. For the most part, opportunities will not come looking for you. You'll have to recognize them when they present themselves, and when they do, you must swing open the door. Opportunities help you grow by allowing you to learn new things. Opportunities:

- Allow you to meet new people.
- Expand your social and professional circles.
- Get you closer to achieving your leadership goals.
- Get you out of your rut of complacency and routine.
- Help you discover new things about yourself.
- Help elevate your visibility.
- Can lead to more opportunities.

Be willing to take risks, and don't let fear consume you. That said, get out of your own way. Make courage your superpower, step outside your comfort zone, and accept the challenge. Truth is, some of us may be uncomfortable asking for help. It's not something we're particularly conditioned to do, since we may tend to feel we need to do it all. However, when it comes to opportunities at work, if you don't have all the answers, reach out for help. Reach out to a mentor, someone on your success team, a member in your professional or industry organization, or anyone else who can help provide you with the information or knowledge you need to support your new project. Do your research. It's okay if you don't have all the answers. Prepare, study, and create a plan of action to ensure you have everything you need to achieve a positive outcome. The important thing here is that you say yes.

Also, let your boss know that you're interested in new opportunities. Being proactive sends a message that you're ready to step up your game and take your talent and skills to the next level. Good for you!

Job seekers don't need to have all the answers either. For example, if you see a job posting and you don't meet all the requirements listed on the job description, apply for it anyway. According to a survey by Robert Half, a global staffing firm, "62 percent of employees have been offered a job when they didn't match the exact qualifications," and "84 percent of companies are willing to hire and train a candidate who lacks required skills."[*] Besides, if there's nothing new to learn from a new position, and no new skills to acquire, you may not want that job anyway, unless you feel it's a company with a culture you think would be a better fit, or that would move you closer to your leadership goals.

Seize opportunities even if you don't have all the answers. Most importantly, don't be afraid to make mistakes. Even if your efforts don't have the desired results, you ultimately learn from the experience. Don't take

---

[*] Robert Half, "Survey: 42 Percent of Job Applicants Don't Meet Skills Requirements, but Companies Are Willing to Train Up," *PR Newswire,* March 19, 2019.

disappointments or missteps personally. Detach from them and develop resilience so you can evaluate mistakes, see where you went wrong, and bounce back. You have nothing to be ashamed of. It's not a reflection of who you are; it's a part of life. If this happens to you, be open about what went wrong and share your experiences with others. Vulnerability is a sign of strength, not weakness. As they say, pick yourself up, dust yourself off, and try again. These people did:

- Thomas Edison is said to have made nine thousand attempts before he perfected the light bulb.
- Michael Jordan was cut from his high school basketball team because of his supposed lack of skill.
- J. K. Rowling was rejected by twelve major publishing houses before one decided to publish her first Harry Potter book.

So don't be afraid to take advantage of opportunities. You don't need all the answers; all you need is to take a prudent risk, throw on your superhero cape, and unleash your superpower—courage—and fly!

SHOUT-OUTS
. . . .

"In leadership roles you have to be OK not knowing things, being vulnerable and willing to learn. That's how you grow."

—Viola Davis

. . . .

"I'd rather regret the risks that didn't work out than the chances I didn't take at all."

—Simone Biles

. . . .

"I'm always the one to ask the second and third questions."

—Thasunda Brown Duckett

Have the Audacity to Put Yourself Out There

If you keep doing the same thing over and over,
you'll keep getting the same results. Where there is no discomfort,
there is no growth, and you remain in a state of complacency.

As a leader, stepping outside your comfort zone is not an option—it's required. No ifs, ands, or buts. Trying new things is essential to your growth, and exposure to new situations and new people can propel you and your career forward to new heights. Explore other cultures and different social and industry events to increase your exposure to new things and gain access to new people and new opportunities for personal, professional, and leadership growth.

Think back to when you've done something that scared you. Your heart started racing, your breathing changed, self-doubt and anxiety took over, your palms turned sweaty anticipating the unknown. Maybe it was making a presentation or accepting a job relocation. But you decided to take a risk and overcame your fears. Remembering these experiences is key to developing self-confidence, and feeling good about your decision to change is foundational to trying it again.

No matter how much you've grown—whether you've gotten several title promotions or crossed important milestones at your job (or on the calendar!)—it's important to continue to put yourself out there. Navigating the unfamiliar will become more comfortable and help you remove any emotional blocks, like fear of failure, so that it will become easier for you to try something new next time. Complacency is not the place for you.

Having the audacity to put yourself out there is significant because it means you're adaptable and open to change. You're learning to trust yourself in new situations. In this post-pandemic environment when in-person professional encounters may be limited and online communication is more common, stepping outside your comfort zone may mean turning your camera on and accepting that you belong in the room. It could also mean speaking up when you have questions, or sharing your point of view.

There are ways you can put yourself out there strategically. Decide what you want your personal brand to be and what you want to be known for. Then develop ways to demonstrate the skills and strengths that align with your values. For example, starting off with strong phrases like "in my opinion" or "based on my experience" will help to establish your expertise and leadership skills.

Successful leaders often share how important it is to be a lifelong learner—always open to acquiring new skills and insights. Remember, sticking with what you already know will keep you where you already are. If you are concerned about making mistakes, think of them as opportunities to learn and grow. Develop the mindset that any obstacle can be considered either a stumbling block or a stepping stone. Your attitude will determine which it will be. If you avoid the things that scare you, you'll never learn new things. Even if you consider yourself to be an introvert, lead with your strengths and push yourself to accept new challenges. Take small steps. It gets easier with time, and unexpected paths often lead to rewarding destinations.

. . . .

"Put on your big-girl panties."

"You'll never know until you try."

SHOUT-OUT
. . . .

"I am lucky that whatever fear I have inside me,
my desire to win is always stronger."

—Serena Williams

Mastering New Technologies to Enhance Your Leadership Skills

*It is never too late to learn new skills or go back to school
to increase your work options and opportunities.
Many employers now consider skills as well as educational attainment.*

Nuew and emerging technologies are impacting every industry and all our lives. Artificial intelligence, blockchain, robotics, cybersecurity: these have changed the way we all live and work—and that's just in the past few decades! It is imperative to find ways to welcome these advances into our lives and careers.

When used effectively, technologies can enhance communications, improve workflows, strengthen supply chains, improve quality control, personalize and enhance the customer experience, and increase collaboration to make businesses, organizations, schools, and governments more productive and efficient. Whether we like it or not, technologies are reshaping our future.

Both emerging leaders and experienced executives have embraced new inventions as components of their personal lives and leadership strategies. While we may be less comfortable with new instruments and digital resources, we recognize the critical need to step out of our comfort zones and learn how to employ these technologies so as to be effective in managing our teams and workflows.

The most effective and impactful leaders will overcome their fears and frustrations about the constantly changing technologies that are impacting our lives. Whether you consider yourself to be new-school or old-school, you must learn to master innovative tools that will enhance your leadership skills and develop you both personally and professionally. You can improve your personal technological intelligence and tech readiness on a regular basis by asking others to share their tech knowledge with you and others. You can also upgrade your team's skill sets, expand their thinking, and assuage the fears spawned by technological advances.

Recommendations for embracing technological advances and utilizing them to raise your leadership effectiveness include:

- Incorporate tech experts, developers, influencers, and content creators on your success team, or personal board of directors. They can add fresh perspectives to your worldview and expand your problem-solving strategies.
- Be open to intergenerational and innovative ideas you may receive from younger members of your team, as well as from team members who may be introverts, or not as outgoing as others. They can really boost your comfort levels with advancing technologies and help you find the most effective ways to integrate them into your organization.
- Consider establishing your own research-and-development (R & D) unit, tech team, or chief technology officer (CTO), no matter the size of your organization. You may think your business is too small for such positions, but you cannot afford not to have them.
- Consider hiring a college or graduate school student who may be able to obtain credits from their school as interns or externs. You may also barter or trade the sharing of skill sets and points of view, so that you both benefit from the experience. This reverse mentoring can be very beneficial.

- Invest in courses that introduce you to new technologies that make sense for your industry and, if possible, take advantage of training opportunities in your organization. Look for free or low-cost webinars that offer beginner, intermediate, or advanced classes.
- Encourage a spirit of readiness to welcome the ripples of changes our evolving technologies are creating for the future.
- Invite tech experts to share their expertise with you, your team, co-workers, and others throughout your organization on a regular basis.

. . . .

"The only thing that does not change
is the certainty that everything changes."

SHOUT-OUTS
. . . .

"Don't be afraid to take risks. The greatest rewards
often come from the greatest challenges."

—Mellody Hobson

. . . .

"Even if you think you're gonna make a mistake, that's better than
sitting there quiet because you begin to suffocate . . ."

—Rosalind Brewer

Managing from the Middle, or from Wherever You Are!

You can demonstrate your readiness to advance by leading and influencing others, no matter your current position.

Regardless of your title, position, or place in your organization, you can lead effectively and influentially from wherever you sit or find yourself. Whether you are a project manager, people manager, or process manager, you may feel that you are defined, and perhaps even limited, by your job title, position description, or your place in your organizational hierarchy, but this does not have to be the case. You can show your leadership skills from wherever you are. *You got this!*

First and foremost, you must believe that you can do this. You have to know and affirm your own worth—and the value you bring to any fact-finding, strategic-planning, or decision-making table. You are unique, and along with your authenticity, skill sets, and experience, you can attract attention for achieving successful outcomes and getting results.

Next, you need to do your own job well. Don't get distracted or discouraged by what other people are doing and whether or not someone else—whom you may not feel is more qualified than you—got promoted over you or before you did. It is easy and even understandable to feel resentful or bitter, but those feelings will not help you move forward. To process them, get help from a friend, colleague, or coach if you need to, but focus on doing the job you already have to the best of your ability. Once you have established a reputation for being exceptional at what you do, you can build on that reputational foundation. To be successful, here are skills and attributes to help you manage:

Positive attitude

Effective communication

Listening

Having influence

Relationship building

Ability to negotiate

Ability to motivate

Ability to execute

Problem-solving / conflict resolution

Decision-making

Delegating

Goal setting

Presentation

Team building

Effectively giving feedback

Ability to take criticism or receive feedback

How you manage really matters. All managers are critically important to the success of the organization. You interact with several levels within your business and, in many cases, outside it as well. You may not get all the credit you deserve, but you'll get results for being a stronger leader, and you will learn from the experience.

Once you are known for your excellent work—ethic, habits, and outputs—you can begin to raise your hand for other projects or assignments. You can volunteer to work on or lead a project that is a new mission for your organization. The mission may be one that has not been considered before, or it may involve revisiting an older model to rethink or restructure it on the basis of new ideas and/or new technologies. Whatever the challenge, show up for it!

You might also consider taking an assignment that no one else wants. While there may be good reasons that a project has stalled or become dormant, you may have fresh perspectives and be able to blaze a trail to success, or at least get the ball rolling.

Be thoughtful about how to showcase your leadership skills and abilities. Look for opportunities within your organization that will not drown or dwarf you, and that will give you chances to work and collaborate across divisions or business units, so that you can add to your skill sets by learning more about how your organization functions while gaining visibility.

The leadership roles you hold outside of your job—in your church, your sorority, or other community service organizations—can also bolster your ability to lead, manage, and influence from your current position. You may not realize how multifaceted you already are.

However you decide to proceed as a manager, first believe in yourself, do your own job well, then look for ways that are outside your comfort zone to feature your outstanding leadership abilities. Volunteer to do new things. Be your own best agent, and you will attract other advocates, mentors, sponsors, and promoters.

....

"Strut your stuff!"

"Management is doing things right.
Leadership is doing the right things."

SHOUT-OUT
....

"Start with the end in mind."

—Stephen Covey

13

Working Effectively with Diverse Teams

With Gen-Xers, millennials, and boomers now working together, learn
how best to utilize the team to maximize creativity and productivity.

B y now it's well documented that diverse teams drive better performance and revenue. A McKinsey & Company study, "Diversity
Matters" (2015), showed that "companies in the top 25% for racial/eth-
nic and gender diversity were respectively 36% and 25% more likely to
have superior financial returns."* However, working with diverse people
in diverse teams can present challenges. How do you get a mixed group
of different generations, races, genders, and socioeconomic status, with
cross-cultural and/or global backgrounds, to work better together and
appreciate and respect one another's differences?

Inclusion is the goal. People need to feel included in order to be productive and see themselves as part of a team. And for that to happen,
their opinions must be heard, and their contributions must be valued. It
may be somewhat natural to gravitate toward and bond with those who
are similar to you; however, as a good leader and team member, you
should develop an attitude of curiosity. Sharing and learning about the
experiences of others from different cultures and backgrounds are how

---

* "Why Diversity and Inclusion Are Good for Business," University of North Carolina at
Pembroke, October 27, 2021.

you can work better with others on a diverse team—and how to be better at leading one.

Working effectively with diverse teams, whether you're on a team or leading one, is more critical now than ever. Here are some tips to help you shift your mindset, behaviors, and practices.

If you're on a diverse team:

1. Find ways to make your teammates feel valued.
2. Show teammates you appreciate and respect their differences.
3. Identify someone on your team who is different than you as a mentor you can learn and benefit from; or perhaps you can offer yourself as a mentor so they can learn from you.
4. Ask your teammates for ideas and feedback that may be different from your own.
5. Ask others what resources are available to provide you with new learning and opportunities so you can enhance your skills or upskill.
6. Suggest that team members take turns sharing their stories at the top of meetings so that they can get to know one another.

If you're leading a diverse team:

1. Communicate your vision and expectations for collaboration.
2. Make your employees feel valued and appreciated.
3. Show respect for everyone's cultural differences.
4. Provide developmental and learning opportunities, and other tools your team may need to be successful.
5. Encourage mentoring among team members to avoid a sense of competitiveness.
6. Identify and eliminate any biases with expert training if needed.

7. Get feedback and constructive criticism from individuals and the team as a whole so they feel they have ownership and a stake in the team's development and success.

Today, diverse teams may include four generations of workers now active in the workplace: baby boomers, Generation X, millennials, and Generation Z. As a refresher, it may be helpful to recognize that each generation has its unique characteristics, style of working, and approach to getting the job done. Here are commonly accepted descriptions of categories of various generations:

> **Baby boomers:** born between 1946 and 1964. Tend to be loyal to their employers, self-motivated, have a strong work ethic, competitive.
>
> **Generation X:** born between 1965 and 1980. Tend to be efficient, direct in communication style, adaptable to new technologies, dependable.
>
> **Millennials:** born between 1981 and 1996. Tend to be competitive, achievement-oriented, tech savvy, focused on work-life balance. (Comprise the biggest group in the workforce.)
>
> **Generation Z:** born between 1997 and 2012. Tend to need autonomy, well-versed in social media, digital natives, self-directed. (This group has never known a world without the internet. It's also the most ethnically and socioeconomically diverse generation in the corporate workforce.)

Regardless of our generational tendencies, inclusion is paramount in making organizational teams stronger and more effective. Being sensitive to some generational hallmarks can support an inclusive approach. For example, because of the COVID-19 pandemic and global quarantine practices, many members of Generation Z have had radically different academic and work life experiences than their millennial and Gen X counterparts. Forced into remote learning, many graduated high school online instead of onstage. When they got to college, many were unable to have traditional on-campus experiences and in-person interactions with other students and professors. Social media and texting became the preferred way of communication. For this group, *remote* became the norm. Being at home became the norm. We all have to be better, do better, and strive better to work together. The pandemic challenged all of us in one way or another, and it's up to us to work effectively in diverse teams and to lead diverse teams effectively to be successful.

....

"Great minds, young and old,
can come together and achieve great things."

SHOUT-OUTS

"If you want to go fast, go alone.
If you want to go far, go together."

—African proverb

....

"Talent wins games, but teamwork and
intelligence win championships."

—Michael Jordan

Managing a Global Workforce

The challenges of managing a global workforce are evolving as our economies, technologies, and environments continue to change. We must adapt our leadership strategies to be inclusive and inspirational.

You may already be responsible for managing and/or participating in a workforce that includes people from other cities, other countries, or even other continents. While such diverse work cultures can produce strong results, they can also be difficult to relate to, work with, and lead. How can you make sure that you get the most from your global teams?

Here are some recommended strategies:

1. Get to know the countries and cultures that your workforce members are from.
   * If you have not or cannot visit the countries yourself, reach out to the liaisons to those places within your organizations or others who may be familiar with the region. Find out how these employees were recruited, hired, and on-boarded.
   * Consider expanding your own cultural capabilities. Do you speak the language of one or more of the countries where you now manage or interact with workers? Are you interested in learning more about those cultures? If so,

don't be shy about asking questions and demonstrating your interest.

- What are their special strengths and skill sets? Are there particular differences about their work hours, schedules, holidays, and/or beliefs that could impact the cohesiveness of your team?
- How much do they know about the mission and culture of your organization? Do they understand how their work contributes to the bottom line?
- Consider hiring or working with consultants who specialize in cultural fluency. This field has arisen to support cross-cultural workforces in all genres.

2. Make sure your team members meet one another.

- Conduct regular meetings at times that work for everyone, and/or rotate meeting dates and times so that no one group of people is impacted more heavily than others.
- Introduce members of the team and give them opportunities to share information about themselves, their roles, and how they can add strength to the team. As new members join the team, be sure to include them in introductions.
- Consider rotating meeting leadership or featured speaking responsibilities, particularly if diverse team members can share substantive information that can be helpful.

3. Get to know the countries and cultures that your clients/ customers are from.

- Sometimes the client or customer base is different from the countries or cultures of the workers providing products and/or services to them. Make sure team members have thoroughly explored the possible alignments or misalignments of the countries and cultures involved and matched the most effective and efficient suppliers of products and services with their clients/consumers.

4. Make sure that all team members know as much as possible about the cultures of the clients they are serving.

   • Include cross-cultural information and training in your team preparations, so that they can be ready to acknowledge and employ the special skill sets available among their diverse team members to better serve the unique needs of their clients and customers.

5. Cultivate an atmosphere of respect for every country and culture represented on the team and in your client/customer base.

   • Respecting the unique interests, skills, backgrounds, and communication styles of the workforce, colleagues, customers, and clients can elevate the quality and quantity of your work output.

6. Include regular reviews and assessments of and updates on your global workforce communications policies and procedures so that you can respond quickly to changes in the geographical areas where the workforce is found, whether political, environmental, or other.

7. Look for opportunities to collaborate across divisional, organizational, and cultural differences to build the strongest teams that you can.

. . . .

"When we each bring something different to the table,
it makes the table richer, more beautiful, and stronger."

SHOUT-OUTS
. . . .

"To prepare the workforce, you have to understand the world."

—Tae Yoo

. . . .

"The strength of the team is each individual member.
The strength of each member is the team."

—Phil Jackson

15

Don't Get It Twisted: Followers May Be Liked, but Leaders Are Respected

Everyone wants to be liked, but in leadership,
it's better to be respected.

There is a shift that occurs when you rise to the ranks of leadership status. As you distance yourself from day-to-day responsibilities and focus on vision and big-picture strategy, your concern is less about others liking you and more about gaining respect. Leadership is not about being crowned Ms. Popularity. Leaders are not people pleasers. Leadership is about making difficult decisions, holding others accountable, and providing critical feedback so that you can make an impact to achieve company goals and objectives.

As an effective leader, you'll have to solve problems and deliver results that won't make everyone happy. While being liked is an important tool in leadership that fosters open communication and collaboration and creates a comfortable and productive work environment, it should not come at the expense of your authority and your ability to make tough decisions.

Ideally, there should be a balance between likeability and respect—knowing when to cultivate a rapport with individuals and when to exert authority. It's important to use your emotional intelligence and connect with teams on a personal level to inspire and build trust, but your priority is not to make others feel good and for them to like you. Your job is to make the best choices for your team and department, for the right reasons, so you make a positive impact—especially when the going gets tough, like it or not.

....

"People trust leaders they respect."

"Having lots of *likes* doesn't make you an effective leader."

SHOUT-OUT

"A leader is one who knows the way, goes the way, and shows the way."

—John C. Maxwell

16

Always Have a Plan of Action and Follow Through

Goal setting, executing against those goals,
and holding yourself accountable is the way to get ahead.

In order to really be effective, goals (sometimes labeled *intentions*) should be documented—in writing or digitally—and reviewed regularly. To make your goals meaningful requires you to reflect and be honest with yourself and take into account *what* you want to accomplish and *why* this is important to you personally, and then to set a time frame for *when* you want to accomplish the goals you set. The best place to do this is in what we call your Personal Leadership Notebook, or PLN.

Your PLN can be any notebook devoted to keeping track of the immediate, short-term, long-term, and legacy goals that you set along your leadership journey—any special projects or assignments and the results; new strategies you put into place; any accolades received from your boss, co-workers, clients, or customers; any awards received; your own reflections, inspirational quotes, graphics, or visuals that chronicle your accomplishments throughout the year and reminded you of how hardworking and fabulous you are. Keep in mind that your goals may change as life changes, and that's okay.

You can also use your PLN for personal goals, like a commitment to weekly exercise, trying out a new recipe once a week or per quarter, or professional goals, like attending a monthly networking event or registering for a webinar. Goals should be specific, clear, measurable, and timely. They should help develop a road map for actions that direct us toward our desired outcome. This doesn't mean that we will never go off course, but clear goals will help with making decisions, setting boundaries, allocating time for priorities, and seeing opportunities that we may otherwise have overlooked. Clearly articulating these goals and road map can serve as motivation and an accountability tool, reminding us to celebrate achievements, large or small, to review how far we have come, to tweak our strategies and methods, and to easily review what still needs to be done.

For some leaders, personal and professional goal setting can, and often does, get disregarded because of fear. Fear of failure and fear of accountability to ourselves and others can derail us, especially during these busy, unpredictable times. However, once you make goal setting a habit, you may find it rewarding, fun, and confidence building.

As an example, try setting goals in different parts of your life—career, health, family, relationships, travel, etc. Then think of one thing you want to do, try, or experience in the areas you list and by when. (Google "Wheel of Life" to see various templates for ideas.)

Regardless of your preferred tool—PLN, Wheel of Life, or any other goal-setting aid—use it and refer to it habitually. Not setting goals allows someone else to set the direction of your career and life for you, and you don't want that to happen!

. . . .

"Don't just think about it, do it!"

SHOUT-OUTS

"If you aim at nothing, you will reach it every time."

—B. J. Marshall

. . . .

"The tragedy of life does not lie in not reaching your goals. The tragedy lies in not having any goals to reach."

—Dr. Benjamin E. Mays

How to Manage Your
Emotional Self and Keep It All Together

Developing good relationships with co-workers has more benefits than you think, so control and learn from your emotions to increase emotional intelligence.

I f you think your IQ is what will get you promoted, or that how well you excel at your job will get you that raise, you may be only half right. Experts say it's your *emotional intelligence*—how you manage yourself and your relationships—that will get you noticed. EI has to do with being aware of your emotions and those of others. EI consists of four key components: self-awareness, self-management, social awareness, and relationship management. Empathy is at the core of emotional intelligence and is defined as the ability to appreciate and understand how another person feels. It's commonly known that many careers are derailed for reasons related to emotional competencies, such as unsatisfactory team leadership during times of difficulty or conflict. Having empathy in the workplace is considered a highly rated leadership skill, and many employers value that more than technical skills.

To test your EI, ask yourself the following questions:

Do I stay calm under pressure?
Do I have empathy and compassion for my co-workers and others?

Can I effectively find strategic and creative ways to resolve
conflict?

Do I listen and try to see situations as others see them?

Do I connect with others on a personal level?

Do I show kindness in the workplace?

Am I respectful even though I may disagree with others?

Do I keep a level head even though things may not go my way?

If you answered yes to all these questions, consider yourself to have
high EI. However, if you didn't answer yes to these questions, you should
reflect on what you should do to raise your emotional intelligence, and
note how you are possibly being perceived and evaluated. Remember,
the first person you lead is yourself.

Emotional intelligence can be learned, practiced, and improved. To
lead a team, you must be self-aware. In order to bring out the best in
people, you have to bring out the best in yourself.

As a leader, showing empathy allows your team members and colleagues to feel like they're in a safe space where they can be free to fully
engage, share their thoughts, and express ideas to maximize productivity. This is how you build a stronger team.

Now that the world has changed and many workplaces are remote and
hybrid, demonstrating emotional intelligence can be challenging. The
fact is, many of us may no longer have face-to-face contact on a regular
basis, and when we do go into an office, sometimes we don't have assigned workspaces. Moving to a different desk every day or straddling
work environments and managing relationships can be stressful and
frustrating, especially if our geography has changed and we no longer
live where we work.

Online platforms can be a hotbed of miscommunication, where sig-
nals are crossed and body language is misinterpreted. It might be easy
to lose patience when your only point of contact is a tiny box on a small

screen and you're trying to get your point across, make a connection, or establish a rapport.

Count to ten, take a deep breath, pause, and ask or rephrase a question to make sure you and your team are on the same page and everyone is being understood. Say, "Help me understand," so that you can get clarification. Or if you feel you need to research an issue, let others know you'll get back to them with more information, and then follow up. If you don't have your own office or desk, find a space to have a private conversation so you can come to a resolution or an understanding. Maintaining good relationships is still key.

The same rules apply for emotional intelligence in the virtual world as they do in face-to-face communications. Because you may not be physically working in the same space, you'll have to find strategic and creative ways to connect and manage your emotions and the emotions of others.

Being able to express emotions is important for everyone, but being able to think, connect our mind to our emotions, and manage them is what turns us into leaders. So hold it down, and keep yourself together.

SHOUT-OUTS
· · · · · · · · · · · · · · · · · ·

"Learning to stand in somebody else's shoes,
to see through their eyes, that's how peace begins.
And it's up to you to make that happen. Empathy is a
quality of character that can change the world."

—Barack Obama

· · · · · · · · ·

"I've learned that people will forget what you said,
people will forget what you did,
but people will never forget how you made them feel."

—attributed to Maya Angelou

. . . .

"Being able to express our emotions is human,
but being able to think, connect our mind to our
emotions and manage them is what turns us into leaders."

—Daniel Goleman

Developing Yourself and Others

Reimagine a new work environment where you share your visionary leadership by developing your management skills while motivating others to develop and utilize their strengths.

L eaders should consistently try to better themselves and their approach to situations they encounter. As emerging and established leaders, we must continue to look for ways to develop *ourselves* while we develop those around us.

This requires being open to learning new skills and creating a supportive learning environment for others. To do this, you must be an active listener: hear what others need and build a foundation of trust. As you step outside your comfort zone and take prudent risks, encourage others to try new things as well. Remaining open to learning new things is key.

Formal education such as additional degrees, certifications, or professional courses and webinars can be beneficial, as can informal learning and tapping into ways to convert our inner power into influence. Power is something we have, and influence is something we do when we need to share ideas that bring others over to understanding our position or point of view, or invite others to take action.

As work environments change, so do the needs of the organization, so looking for gaps and trends that are not being addressed can be a developmental exercise resulting in increased visibility and possible advancement within our companies. Don't think that because something has not been done before, it cannot be done. Think of the skills you have and want to enhance, or new skills you would like to acquire, and encourage others to do the same. Good leaders motivate those around them by seeing, listening, and utilizing and playing up their strengths.

As you cultivate your "learning mode," use your voice in forums both inside and outside work such as panels, social media, group discussions, etc. Don't be shy about making suggestions and addressing challenges based on what you've learned. Offer viable solutions rather than just identifying problems, and encourage others to do the same. Sometimes, just offering possible suggestions brings positive visibility, demonstrates an open mindset, and can lead to opportunities.

As Toni Morrison famously said, "The function of freedom is to free someone else," so as you grow, consider how you can become a mentor to others around you. Share information, resources, books, articles, and tools that have helped you along the way and might be useful to those working alongside you. Perhaps plan a gathering on a regular basis where you can share ideas from these resources and even implement a few strategies you've learned that you feel make good business sense.

Also, seek a mentor for yourself who can help guide your personal and professional development. Lead by example and foster growth by sharing your knowledge and new ideas. By adopting these strategies, we not only develop ourselves, but we also create environments at work and within our communities where leadership, influence, and accountability are nurtured and celebrated.

To develop yourself and others at the same time can seem to be a bit daunting, but here is where negotiating and time-management skills come into play—skills that are essential in any setting, and especially important in leadership.

....

"Schedule time to reevaluate your development."

SHOUT-OUTS

"Success isn't about how much money you make;
it's about the difference you make in people's lives."

—Michelle Obama

. . . .

"Before you are a leader, success is all about growing yourself.
When you become a leader, success is all about growing others."

—Jack Welch

19

Emphasizing Self-Care

Demonstrate self-care—for mental health, physical health,
and spiritual health—and use it as a tool to survive and thrive.
Always try to maintain balance.

A s Black women, it's imperative to put ourselves at the top of our to-do lists when it comes to our mental, physical, and spiritual health, and that includes rest. If we don't take care of our health, we won't be able to do our best work and show our best leadership potential.

Buying into the myth of the strong Black woman—that we have to work harder than everyone else, that we have to do everything ourselves and not ask for help, compounded by the effects of institutional racism and discrimination—can deplete our energy and take a toll on our mental and physical health.

According to Erica Martin Richards, MD, PhD, in an article for Johns Hopkins Medicine entitled *Mental Health Among African American Women,* "Women are at least twice as likely to experience an episode of major depression as men. Compared to their Caucasian counterparts, African American women are only half as likely to seek help."

If you feel you are suffering or struggling with your mental health, you owe it to yourself to seek help and support. You may not always be able to find a therapist who looks like you, but search for one you feel comfortable with to talk to about what you're going through. Group therapy could be a more affordable option, or start your own circle of friends group for support. Social circles among women you trust are an important way to find solutions, solve problems, talk through issues, and relieve stress. Also, most mid- to large-size companies offer employees mental health benefits through employee assistance programs, but some studies show that many of us don't access or take advantage of these programs either because we don't make the time or due to stigma, embarrassment, or shame. Needing help for mental illness is not a sign of weakness; it's a sign of strength and nothing to be ashamed of. We check in with a doctor for what ails us physically, and we also need to seek professional help for anything troubling our minds.

It goes without saying that our physical health is just as important as our mental health. Due to preexisting health conditions, healthcare disparities, and lack of healthcare resources in certain parts of the country, Black people were dying from COVID-19 at higher rates than others at the beginning of the pandemic. As a result, our eyes were opened to the lifesaving benefits of maintaining good physical health. Heart disease is still the number-one killer of Black women. In addition to medication and a healthy diet, regular daily physical activity can help lower the risk of high blood pressure, high cholesterol, type 2 diabetes, and stroke. Even making time for something as simple as regular walking, yard work, or playing your favorite music and dancing count toward lowering the risk of these diseases. Joining a fitness club and actually going, working out to YouTube exercise videos on your phone or computer from the comfort of your home, or signing up for a fitness group can help change your life by preventing and even reversing some illnesses. We need to take care of ourselves mentally, physically, and, of course, spiritually.

Spirituality and religious attendance and practices have historically been the foundation of our existence so we could *keep on keeping on* and *make a way out of no way.* Whatever your beliefs, whether they be in God or a higher power, a daily practice of reading scripture, reciting mantras or affirmations, deep breathing, or meditating—all are associated with positive health outcomes and are part of the self-care we need to help us achieve our goals. But self-care is not just about achieving and being active. We must also include rest. The state of rest plays a vital role in our self-care. Because of the stereotype that Black people are lazy, along with the transgenerational trauma we may carry from the enslavement of our ancestors who worked ten to fourteen hours a day, six days a week, from sun up to sun down, we may also feel like we have to keep going in order to be productive. So today we may find ourselves running on a hamster wheel, thinking we have to keep doing in order to produce more to be successful so we can be perceived as valuable to our bosses and companies. Yet rest is essential to our self-care and well-being, because burnout is real.

In her groundbreaking book *Rest Is Resistance,* Tricia Hersey, founder of The Nap Ministry, talks about the four tenets of the Rest Is Resistance movement. Tenet 3 is "Naps provide a portal to imagine, invent, and heal." Typically, rest is underrated, but our bodies should not be sleep deprived. Taking naps, even catnaps, is perfectly fine, and breaks are required on this journey. We need rest to recharge, to be refreshed and renewed. The state of rest is when we can open our minds to daydream, to receiving new information and ideas.

In addition to naps, rest can also come in the form of yoga, walking on a treadmill, singing in a choir, knitting a scarf, painting a room or a canvas—anything associated with taking a break, giving your mind a chance to relax so it is not thinking about work, meeting deadlines, family, or social obligations. Rest is all about you and should be incorporated into your daily life and scheduled on your calendars. Rest may also include limiting your social media.

We need to shut down and turn off and create a space for ourselves to just be. Rest also means protecting your peace by not engaging with people who drain your energy. Self-care is not optional. It's not a luxury; it's a must. And you must put you at the top of your to-do list; this will allow you to put your best foot forward.

SHOUT-OUTS
· · · · · · · · · · · · · · · · · · ·

"Self-care is how you take your power back."

—Lalah Delia

· · · · · · · · ·

"If you prioritize yourself you are going to save yourself."

—Gabrielle Union

· · · · · · · · ·

"We must believe we are worthy of rest.
We don't have to earn it. It is our birthright.
It is one of our most ancient and primal needs."

—Tricia Hersey

20

Keep Your Own Spirits Up

Even during challenging times, motivate yourself while working with others. To attain victory, stay positive.

As a leader, you will experience many challenging times: dealing with office politics, managing various personalities, motivating and influencing others, shifting leadership styles based on the circumstances, changing priorities, meeting deadlines, supporting corporate and company mandates. Needless to say, all of the above can be exhausting. However, in spite of all this juggling, and through all the ups and downs, it's important to have a positive mindset to keep your spirits up. In today's business landscape, effective leadership does not only include good skills, it also includes a positive mindset and leadership presence. Your mindset as a leader shapes your actions, your decision-making, and your overall impact within your organization. Your mind is a valuable tool, and you're on this journey for the long haul, so keep a steady pace while on this track. A positive attitude is what you'll need to reap the rewards.

Countless studies have demonstrated that a positive mindset has many benefits. It can help you live longer and decrease depression and anxiety. It reduces stress, and it helps you stay more open to building relationships, think more clearly to overcome obstacles, and be more creative and open to ideas. Having a positive mindset will attract more positive people to you, and these are the folks you'll want to have around you to provide you with support.

Having a positive attitude starts with swapping out a negative thought with a positive one. Change negative self-talk to positive self-talk. This will take practice if you're a glass-is-half-empty kind of person, but you can do it. For example:

Negative Self-Talk	Strategies to Achieve Positive Self-Talk
There is no way I can get this assignment done on time.	Time management. Think about how long the assignment will take, and break it into manageable chunks to meet your deadline.
Despite my good work, I don't think I'll ever be promoted.	What are you trying to get promoted to? Focus on the skills required to demonstrate that you're ready.
I don't know how to lead a remote or hybrid team.	Look for people who are doing it successfully and learn from them.
I don't believe I have enough resources to finish this project.	First, define what resources you think you need. Then negotiate for people, time, or money *or* look for options to modify the project and/or ask for flexibility.

Don't be managed by your (negative) feelings. If you have a negative thought, put a pin in it. You can choose how you respond to situations and circumstances. Remember, it's not the circumstances but how you react to the circumstances that will determine the outcome. In other words, you may not be able to change office politics, departmental decisions, or company culture, but you can change how you experience them. Keeping your spirits up depends on your outlook, not your job. When life gives you lemons, make lemonade. Keep optimism and a can-do attitude in the face of adversity.

Besides positive self-talk, here are a few ways to keep your spirits up:

* Daily positive affirmations
* Getting enough sleep and rest
* Drinking lots of water to stay hydrated so your body can function at its best
* Being mindful of healthy nutrition by using protein bars, nuts, and seeds for a quick snack or energy boost
* Stretching for five minutes a few times a day
* Doing a few chair or standing exercises to get your oxygen flowing while you work

If you have a religious or faith-based practice, find ways to engage it routinely, to meditate and be thankful, showing gratitude for the blessings you surely have received and for the blessings yet to come.

Just as you need to keep your spirits up, set the example and allow opportunities for your team to keep their spirits up too. Let them be heard, share their feelings, ask questions, and discuss concerns. Play a little music at the top of a meeting to set the tone so that team members can relax, or ask someone to share a positive story that happened to them that day or that week, and it doesn't have to be work related. These small gestures can set the tone for your team to keep the conversation positive and productive.

Positive thinking means approaching unfavorable situations in a more positive, productive, and constructive way. Lifting your spirits up will take effort, patience, and practice, so be kind to yourself and practice positive self-talk until it becomes a habit. Focus more on the things you can control and less on the things you can't. Keep working and living your best life, and try to always look on the bright side. A positive attitude and mindset will likely lift your spirits and put you on the road to positive outcomes along your leadership journey.

....

"A positive outlook can attract positive people,
experiences, and outcomes in your life."

SHOUT-OUTS

"Change your thoughts and you can change your world."

—Norman Vincent Peale

....

"Positive thinking is a valuable tool that can help you
overcome obstacles, deal with pain, and reach new goals."

—Amy Morin

21

Coaches Are Not Just for Athletes: They Can Help You Too

To help you navigate forward, a coach can provide strategies, identify blind spots, and be a great source of support in helping you achieve your professional and personal goals.

The best professionals in any given craft accept input, feedback, and guidance from their coach. We know that in sports, coaches help athletes improve their game. Yet successful business professionals who may work with a coach at different times in their career, and have received the benefits, are sometimes reluctant to share this information.

A coach can be hired at any stage of your career: early development, midcareer, senior leadership, retirement, starting a new venture, or pursuing other life goals. There is no best time to ask for and accept assistance.

It is important to understand why a coach can be important to your career.

This person:

- Offers constructive, unbiased feedback.
- Helps clarify personal and professional goals.
- Offers encouragement and motivation.
- Helps develop strategies to market your strengths.
- Suggests opportunities within and outside your organization.
- Helps develop a positive mindset.

- Offers valuable insights and networking opportunities.
- Helps talk through and analyze complex situations.
- Offers insights on handling emotional triggers.
- Helps develop strategies to move forward.
- Ensures confidentiality and a safe space.
- Holds you accountable and helps you stay on track.

We all have blind spots. It is easy to do what we have always done and remain in our comfort zones and hard to know how to get out of our comfort zones without help from someone else. To grow and be successful as a leader, we should take into account not only what we do well but also areas that can or should be handled differently. Remember, leadership and learning go hand and hand. As we grow, situations change, and getting input from a trusted source can prove invaluable. The best professionals, no matter the industry or field they are in, should accept input and guidance from a coach. You owe it to yourself. Why Not You?

Your coach should be one that listens to your ideas, asks probing questions, and helps to develop strategies to move you toward the goals you desire. A coach does not tell you what to do but offers opinions, judgments, strategies, and feedback that you may not have thought about or heard before. Working with a coach can not only help you navigate your current role but should also help you develop skills needed to navigate future positions.

Being a leader is a demanding job, and a coach can provide support as we navigate the challenges of being in high-profile situations or ones where we want our skills to be more visible. Coaches can also help us with developing emotional intelligence and offer guidance relating to maintaining work-life balance.

Of course, trust is imperative in this relationship. You and your coach must be able to speak freely with each other, and you must be able to accept constructive criticism. You will know you are ready to work with a coach when you are open to and accepting of working differently and learning new strategies and willing to change the way you respond or react in certain situations. A coach should be a thinking partner whom you trust and can openly share ideas with. They can help you flush out ideas and goals and work out the best way to achieve them.

Your coach should be someone whose recommendations you find valuable and who can help you develop a strategic plan in areas that you may not have thought of to amplify your vision and your growth. They can help you map out specific steps toward the goals you have set for yourself. Normally a coach-client relationship is established with a formal agreement, and the coaching services are paid for by the client (you) or your company or organization.

A mentor is someone who is willing to share advice and feedback based on their own experiences. Mentors are usually at a higher level than you and have wide-ranging connections that can expand your network within and outside your organization. They see something in you that they admire and will share ideas to help you modify your thoughts and develop and fine-tune your skill sets. The mentor-mentee relationship is usually informal, and there is no cost.

For clarification:

A Coach: listens to you and helps you make decisions.

A Mentor: talks with you to share their experiences pertaining to a particular situation.

A Sponsor: speaks about you with other decision-makers to help elevate you and advance your career.

You might consider looking for a coach by reaching out to your success team, mentors, sponsors, trusted advisors, and professionals you admire. Think of your coach as another tool in your leadership toolkit, and take advantage of this opportunity whenever possible.

. . . .

"Coaches can be your biggest cheerleaders."

SHOUT-OUTS
. . . .

"Coaching is unlocking a person's potential
to maximize their growth."

—John Whitmore

. . . .

"Does good coaching work? Yes.
Good coaches provide a truly important service.
They tell you the truth when no one else will."

—Jack Welch

22

Respecting the Uniqueness of Others

Being open to listening and learning can lead to deeper trust and
commitment among people from different backgrounds.
Sharing communications and conversations about race, gender,
and culture can bring people closer together, build stronger teams,
and create a more positive work environment.

In the best of situations, you will have the opportunity to recruit,
work with, and/or lead a very diverse team. Research has consistently shown that well-managed, respected, and valued diverse teams
produce powerful results across many different sectors and industries.[*]

It is important to examine your own assumptions about, behaviors
toward, and expectations of your colleagues or team members, and to
learn as much about them as you can. Once you are clearer about what
you do and do not know about them, their skill sets, and the values they
bring, you can tailor your leadership approach as appropriate.

Meeting with your colleagues and teams to share expectations is key
and can help clear up any confusion brought about by misperceptions,
whether yours or theirs. Aligning goals, objectives, strategies, and timelines regularly gives you the chance to refine them as changes occur
within and outside your organization that could impact your plans.

Listening effectively can assist you in determining the expertise and
experience available to help you problem-solve. It is as important to pay

---

* "Why Diversity and Inclusion Are Good for Business," University of North Carolina at
Pembroke, October 27, 2021.

attention to what is *not* being said as it is to be receptive to the ideas that are shared. Where cultural, gender, or age differences, shyness, or introversion may keep some colleagues or employees from putting their ideas forward, be sure to welcome all contributions and approaches and to encourage everyone to participate.

You may notice that some of your colleagues or team members routinely talk or take over conversations, while others sit back or give up after their efforts to be heard are drowned out or criticized by others. You can guard against dominating voices by thanking them for their input and pointedly asking others, particularly those who have not yet spoken, to take part in the discussion. Modeling respect for differing opinions and ideas is a great way to encourage inclusion, and inviting various perspectives to be shared can lead to creative, unprecedented proposals and solutions.

Inviting your colleagues and team members to make presentations or to take turns leading meetings can highlight flexible approaches to the same problem or challenge, so that everyone benefits from the exchange of ideas. Where there is a risk of polarizing positions, consider bringing in a consultant or mediator who can be objective and make sure that all ideas—even apparently opposing views—can be aired, so that there is an opportunity for some common ground to be found.

Sharing your own vulnerability or lack of expertise on a subject and inviting experts to come in to address your group can make it easier for others in your organization to share what they do know or be honest about what they don't know and would like to learn. Virtual, in-house or off-site retreats can help develop trust and respect across differences and strengthen bonds between and among employees.

With emerging technologies quickening the pace of changes in workplaces, flexibility and agility are the hallmarks of effective leadership. Colleagues with multicultural backgrounds, including those who speak more than one language, hail from different parts of the country or world, and/or have a nontraditional career trajectory can be very helpful to your organization.

Welcome diversity in your workplace, and discover the unique perspectives and new approaches that can strengthen how you lead.

....

"Be a 'welcome table' for differing perspectives!"

SHOUT-OUTS

"To handle yourself, use your head;
to handle others, use your heart."

—commonly attributed to Eleanor Roosevelt

....

"Without appreciation and respect for other people,
true leadership becomes ineffective, if not impossible."

—George Foreman

Do Not Let Distractions Throw You Off Course

Social media, a difficult boss, needy co-workers, crazy politics.
Distractions come in many shapes and forms, but don't let them make
you crazy. Keep your sanity and stay strategic.

There's no way around it. Whether you work from home, in an office, or are in a hybrid situation, you're subject to distractions that can impact your productivity. These interruptions can take your attention away from work and your mind off concentration and make you lose focus. The next thing you know, you're not accomplishing what you need to, you're racing to meet deadlines, and the quality of your work may suffer.

Distractions are diversions that can take you off strategy and delay or prevent you from achieving your leadership goals. They come in different forms, and social media may be one of the biggest culprits. In this high-tech world where people are attached to their devices, you may be more likely to check your phone and respond to text messages throughout the day, engage with social networks, browse internet content, and in some cases, especially among the younger generations, watch streaming services.

Working from home increases the potential for distractions with household chores, tending to children, partners, pets, and package deliveries. Plus, when working from home, others may perceive you as not working at all and drop by for impromptu visits that may seem nice at first but, when they add up, can be a misuse of your time. Beware of all these distractions, because they can contribute to your falling behind or not being prepared, or increase your risk for making mistakes.

Co-workers and team members can be a great source of support and collaboration, but when these office neighbors stop by your desk, cubicle, or workspace to chat, it can make it difficult to stay focused and be productive. Seeking advice on a project or work-related issue is one thing; a conversation around a personal issue is another and should be reserved for after hours. (Please read our chapter on the Office Mammy for more information on that.)

Also, be aware of the individual who creates distractions because they want to sabotage your work and deter you from getting it done, and who derail your opportunities for advancement. Sometimes distractions are innocent, but sometimes they are used to intentionally throw you off course.

While it's important to know what goes on in your department and company, keeping up with office politics can be a huge distraction and turn into a part-time job if you let it. Don't allow your worries about other people to interfere with your ability to focus on the work you need to get done to elevate your visibility for leadership opportunities. Of course, pay attention to structural and organizational changes—who gets recognized or promoted, and why—but stay away from time-consuming gossip.

Unfortunately, distractions can also come in the form of a difficult or demanding boss. If your boss has a habit of disrupting you while you're already working on assignments, shifting priorities and putting you on a totally different project, this can also be a type of distraction. Catching you off guard and making you scramble to switch gears to start something completely new can be daunting when it happens on a regular basis. Bosses are not perfect. They may be stressed because of *their* senior management, have unresolved personal issues, exhibit unconscious bias or microaggressive behaviors, or use communication or managerial styles that present themselves as distractions. If you find yourself in any of these situations, here are a few things to consider:

- Try to tune in to your boss and find out what motivates them to make your relationship easier and the workflow more manageable.
- Get clarification on your current projects and other projects that may be coming down the pipeline to have a sense of the workload that lies ahead.
- Schedule brief, regular check-ins for updates and opportunities for feedback so you can anticipate your boss's requests.
- Most importantly, when speaking to your boss, be sure the conversation is results-driven, illustrating how you can be more efficient and effective doing your work, in order to steer clear of negativity and conflict.

Although you won't be able to avoid distractions altogether, you can limit them to put time back on your side. First, be aware of what your distractions are and which ones impact you the most. Once you identify your distractions, limit these interruptions as much as possible. For example, turn off alerts or choose a time of day to turn them on, use headphones if appropriate to reduce unwanted noise, and stay on topic with conversations to keep them short. In order to become a great leader, you must learn how to manage your time wisely so you are not pulled in too many different directions that will hinder your leadership journey.

SHOUT-OUTS
· · · · · · · · · · · · · · · · · ·

"Keep your eyes on the finish line and not on the turmoil around you."

—Rihanna

· · · · · · · · ·

"One way to boost our willpower and focus is to manage our distractions instead of letting them manage us."

—Daniel Goleman

· · · · · · · · ·

"If I didn't fill my schedule with things
I felt were important, other people would fill my schedule
with things they felt were important."

—Melinda Gates

24

Networking in a Virtual World

*Be sure to network outside your comfort zone and
surround yourself with the right people
to build your success team for guidance and support.*

In March 2020, the world got smaller after a virus dubbed COVID-19 appeared and we found ourselves confined to our homes, and the only way to access others was via the internet and phone. In-person networking events turned into face-to-face interactions on small screens, and the strategy for connecting with others shifted in our work and home lives. According to an article in *Forbes,* "Research by professors at the Yale School of Management shows that our professional and personal networks shrunk by about 16% during the pandemic."[*] At first, social media platforms were the only online tools for connecting to others. Arenas opened up in the years that followed, and now networking activities are a mix of in-person, virtual, and hybrid events. Whether you're just starting out, looking for a different job, an entrepreneur, or already in a leadership or management position, making connections is an important part of attracting new opportunities. There are always techniques

---

[*] Rita Trehan, "How to Build a Stronger, More Diverse Post-Pandemic Network," *Forbes,* August 29, 2022.

and opportunities to meet new people, rekindle relationships, and engage with others. Here are fourteen strategies for virtual networking.

1. Embrace technology. Schedule some time every week for online networking to target new contacts and periodically touch base with those already in your network.
2. Be intentional; have a clear goal to connect and stay in touch with others.
3. Update your professional bio, photo, and profile. Let people get to know who you are, but avoid content that's controversial or negative.
4. Based on your brand, identify others in your industry with mutual interests and similar job titles or career paths.
5. Join virtual or in-person networking groups that align with your personal interests or hobbies.
6. If you're looking to change your industry or career, identify and reach out to those who are in companies you are interested in.
7. Post content that establishes you as an authority in the field or content that reflects your values and/or brand.
8. Join online groups—professional associations or business groups. Show up and actively participate.
9. Start your own leadership group to attract like-minded and other professionals to connect over a specific topic or subject.
10. Attend virtual conferences, webinars, and events, many of which are low or no cost.
11. Identify people who work at companies you're interested in and connect with them. Have a specific goal. Do your research beforehand. Your first interaction should not be an "ask."
12. Follow up a few times with others you meet online. Remember, connecting takes time and patience, so don't be discouraged if you do not immediately hear back.

13. If they do respond, remember: following up is important. Figure out what you can do for them. Ask if there's something they need that you might be able to provide.
14. Look for an opportunity to meet in person, if possible.

No matter the many benefits of virtual networking, including convenience and opportunities for cross-industry and global connections, there are benefits to in-person interactions that can't be replicated via a screen or social media. Face-to-face meetings allow you to get a better sense of the room, read body language and facial expressions, and offer opportunities to develop personal connections and lasting impressions. For in-person meetings, business cards with social media handles may be an option. You can make a note on any detail you'd like to remember about the person you met on the back of their business card or wherever there is room, or make a digital note on your phone.

Networking is an ongoing process and is still the best way to advance your career. It's imperative to meet people in your industry with your level of expertise, but even more important to include those who are at a variety of levels, of a different race, gender, or ethnic background, who can share different insights and perspectives and perhaps connect you with new opportunities for leadership.

SHOUT-OUTS
· · · · · · · · · · · · · · · · · ·

"Networking is the number-one unwritten
rule of success in business."

—Sallie Krawcheck

· · · · · · · · ·

"Your network is your net worth."

—Porter Gale

· · · · · · · · ·

"Everybody shake a hand, make a friend."

—Gladys Knight and the Pips

25

Negotiating a Better Salary

When you feel you deserve more money,
get your ducks in a row to make the "ask."

Let's face it. Most of us aren't comfortable when it comes to asking for money, whether we receive a job offer and want to make a counteroffer or we're in our current position with increased responsibility and feel we deserve a raise or we're seeking a promotion to a higher position. In each of these cases, there may be nuances to how we approach the negotiation process. The first step to asking for a better salary is to know your value, know you are worthy, and communicate the reasons you deserve it. For example, just coming to work and being in a job for an extended period of time doesn't justify or entitle you to ask for a better salary. In other words, just showing up and doing your job is not enough. You have to go above and beyond.

So how do we put a price tag on our value and contributions?

Many men are more comfortable than women are when it comes to asking for more money and negotiating better salaries, which is one reason they are often paid much more than we are for doing the same job with the same job title. If you feel you deserve a better salary, now is your time to step up and prepare to make the "ask."

When it comes to interviewing for a job, the optimal time to negotiate is usually when you receive an official job offer—preferably in writing. However, depending on the level of the job, a more experienced candidate may be comfortable negotiating earlier. This is no time to be shy. If you're an introvert, you must be bold and engage in this conversation in order to get the best offer possible. Prepare your negotiation points by doing research so you can base your "ask" on facts and actual market value for positions with your job title, or with similar job responsibilities. Look at industry trends and salary ranges for your job title and position based on national average salaries. Utilize sites such as Indeed or Glassdoor that feature actual salary ranges for a variety of positions to assist you in this process. Take into account the size of the company posting the salary range as well as its geographic location. For example, a *Fortune* 500 corporation might have a higher salary range than a start-up, midsize company, or nonprofit.

In addition, reach out to your own networks, mentors, or those on your success team. While they may not be able to share an actual salary for your position, they may be able to suggest a salary range based on where they work, provide other advice, or point you in the direction of someone else who could be helpful. After doing this homework, create your own high- and low-end range of salary acceptability to support your counteroffer.

Next, make a list of the special skills or certifications you bring to the table. Tell stories and add details around results you've achieved, business challenges you've faced and overcome, goals you've met, and revenue you've helped generate—skills that can be applied to help your new company meet their goals and objectives. You should know what these are beforehand. Refer to your Personal Leadership Notebook, where you have kept track of your successes on projects, problem-solving assignments, accomplishments, feedback, awards, and accolades received from managers, clients, customers, vendors, co-workers, and other departments. Once you've collected the facts for your counter, be confident, and when you begin your negotiations, be flexible with the outcome.

Now is not the time to get emotional. Now is the time to continue to show gratitude and appreciation for the offer and be prepared in the conversation so that you can win. Employers expect candidates to negotiate, so don't hold back. If you've been in your current position for a while and have been handed additional responsibilities (i.e., you are now wearing ten hats instead of five) and feel you deserve a raise, the aforementioned preparation still applies.

Because you have been documenting and writing in your Personal Leadership Notebook, you now have additional projects, assignments, achievements, results, and accolades to add to your talking points that help support the work you have done to meet department and company goals. Identify your most important successes to add to this list. Since you've taken on new responsibilities, another tactic could be suggesting a change in your job title that reflects your new role. This could also help your argument for negotiating a better salary. Bring ideas for the new title and examples of those salary ranges to the discussion. This strategy has worked for us and others many times: a new job title was earned, and more money was received.

There may be circumstances in which your manager agrees that you are deserving of a raise but the company is not in a position to honor an increase. If this is the case, there are other ways to think about the negotiation process that may not always involve salary. For example, you can request an increase in commission, personal time off, flexible work hours, a larger bonus, stock options, money for education, trade classes, and memberships, or other perks and benefits that may be satisfactory to you. You could also ask your manager if you could revisit the ask at a time when business is more favorable. Whatever you do, don't bury the conversation. Keep hope alive.

If you're seeking a promotion to a higher position within your current company, salary increases are typically less than if you were to have that same position switching jobs to another company. Sometimes, internal promotions don't even come with salary increases, but you are entitled to ask and to negotiate for dollars, perks, or benefits just the same. And the time to do this is during the promotion process. It may seem awkward to discuss more money, since you appreciate the opportunity to elevate your position, but you must make the ask, because you have the right to do it anyway. You have nothing to lose and could gain the respect of your employer because now he or she recognizes that you know your value and would prefer not to settle for less.

On the other hand, if your employer is unwilling to negotiate, don't be afraid to walk away and start looking for other opportunities if you feel you are not being acknowledged or rewarded for your talents. We have done this and know of others who have done this as well.

In summary, before asking for a better salary, ask yourself why you deserve a higher salary than the one the employer is offering, then make your case. Do your homework and be confident that what you are asking for is reasonable and fair. Negotiating a better salary earlier in your career can help get your lifetime earning potential on the right track. If you don't make the effort or take the risk, you could be losing income in the long run. You could miss out on saving for a better future, setting aside to buy a vacation or second home, deducting from your paycheck in a company-matched investment plan, paying for your child's education, or booking that lavish vacation you've always dreamed about. So, provide management with solid reasons why they need to pay you more. Put on your big girl panties and go and make the ask! And when you do, and succeed in your mission, pat yourself on the back for a job well done!

....

"If you don't ask, you won't receive."

SHOUT-OUTS
. . . .

"Let us never negotiate out of fear.
But let us never fear to negotiate."

—John F. Kennedy

. . . .

"Show me the money!"

—Cuba Gooding, Jr., in *Jerry McGuire*

26

Leading After Loss

Throughout your life and career, you may be called upon to lead after a great loss—whether it be the death of someone important to you or a different kind of catastrophic change in your circumstances. Despite the emotional hurdles you may need to overcome, you can lead yourself and others forward.

As experienced leaders who plan strategically, we may think that we are fully prepared to shoulder sudden, unexpected changes in our lives and careers. However, life may interrupt our plans.

Loss—whether of the life of a loved one or colleague; our health; our job or business; our property, neighborhood, or community; or another situation—may really knock us for a loop! We have read about or witnessed great losses and changes in our society and in our world—wars, displacements and resettlements of people, pandemics, natural disasters, and much more. We have experienced loss ourselves—of a parent, a child, a spouse, or a close family or team member. All these events have been followed by periods of mourning, growth, and rebuilding. We can learn from our losses and continue to lead.

Loss can be experienced in many ways, and sometimes, what may seem to others to be a small matter is hugely important to us. And yet we are expected to lead ourselves and others through and beyond these losses. How can we do this with grace and dignity?

One definition of loss in the *Oxford English Dictionary* is "suffering resulting in or related to defeat in a game or contest." We know that loss is much more complicated than a defeat in a sport.

In fact, loss and grief can both be associated with occurrences throughout our lives and our careers as leaders and managers. We have probably all experienced losses and navigated our grief journeys as best we could. Loss and grief can deepen our understanding of others and even serve as bridges to work across differences.

How can we lead after or during a great loss? First, we must acknowledge and accept our grief, however painful that might be. Until we accept the truth and depth of our pain, it can continue to recur in our lives and our work in different ways, keeping us from moving forward.

We may need to gather our courage and seek help as we grapple with our feelings. Grief professionals can be supportive, and we may also reach out to spiritual counselors, grief networks, or our trusted family members and friends.

Next, we need to acknowledge our loss and grief publicly, as long as we can do so in a safe way. By sharing the nature and extent of our losses, we can become more human to our team members and colleagues, and we may be surprised by the support and understanding we receive. Allowing ourselves to be vulnerable can sometimes be our greatest strength.

Taking some time away from our regular duties can also be helpful. Grief is an important part of the coping and healing process. We can delegate our leadership responsibilities to trusted team members or colleagues while we gather ourselves.

Treating our minds, bodies, and spirits well is very important during this time. Journaling about our feelings can be healing, and we can also lean on our cherished friends, those "walk through fire" people who will come to be with us, even in our silence. These friends can tell us if we are overworking, in denial, getting sick, or neglecting ourselves or others. Even if we don't have such a friend, we can become one for others. It is a priceless gift.

As we journey on, we may find that our pool of inner strength is deepened, even as we do all that we must do. In this sense, loss and grief—however profound—can become gifts that expand our ability to appreciate what others may be going through. We can use our newfound compassion to reach out to team members and colleagues (even those we do not readily agree with) and find a common interest or experience upon which a bridge of understanding can be built. Accepting our own feelings of loss and grief, and the "punch in the gut" they sometimes cause, can help us to be more patient when unexpected curveballs are thrown at us and our teams.

We can ask, "Where is the opportunity for growth in what we are experiencing?" or "What can we learn from this?" If we look for the life lesson, we may be better able to withstand the pain and discomfort, and help our teams to do so as well. As Maya Angelou references in her book *Wouldn't Take Nothing for My Journey Now*:

> When I sense myself filling with rage at the absence of a beloved, I try as soon as possible to remember that my concerns and questions, my efforts and answers should be focused on what I did or can learn from my departed love. What legacy was left which can help me in the art of living a good life?

While our progress on our journeys of loss and grief may be uneven, our experiences and learnings can move us to be more thoughtful leaders, able to visualize and craft new paths forward.

....

"Where is the lesson? What can we learn?"

SHOUT-OUTS
· · · · · · · · · · · · · · · · · · · ·

"Ain't no shame in holding on to grief,
as long as you make room for other things too."

—Bubbles, *The Wire*

· · · · · · · · ·

"You will heal, and you will rebuild yourself
around the loss you have suffered."

—Elizabeth Kübler-Ross

Managing Career Transitions

Just because you begin your career in one industry doesn't mean you have to stick with it. Industry- and job-hopping are today's norm. Take the leap and make the move an exciting adventure.

Whether you're in your twenties, thirties, forties, or beyond, as we live longer we tend to work longer, and having as many as five or more career transitions can be the norm. Gone are the days when most people stay at one company their entire careers. AI is reshaping jobs and job descriptions that impact the way we work, and we may find ourselves being job-eliminated and needing to find a new position. Many companies have reorganized to create a more horizontal (flat) rather than vertical (hierarchical) environment that may require us to wear multiple hats, and we may experience frustration, work fatigue, or exhaustion and want to look for a position or industry that provides more work-life balance. Or we may simply have other interests. A career transition is seeking an occupation other than your present one. Maybe you have a career in hospitality or education and now want to shift gears, perhaps move into a different industry and work in technology. Whatever your reason for a career shift—a higher salary, better advancement opportunities, more flexibility, or the pursuit of more fulfilling work—the process of making a career change requires preparation and time. It's important for you to be committed, have a plan of action, and be patient.

There's a difference between being prepared for change that is not initiated by you and preparing for a change that you initiate, control, facilitate, and lead. For example, a layoff or a restructuring of your organization are changes that are not initiated by you but can put you in transition, whereas being established in one career for a period of time and deciding you now want a new one puts you in a different type of transition. In the latter case, the decision is yours, and you have an opportunity to prepare. The three of us have had opportunities to prepare for career transitions from various positions and different industries that range from moving out of corporate America to reinventing ourselves and establishing our own businesses, individually and together. There is no one way or right path to making a career change, but here are a few things to help you facilitate a smooth transition and get closer to your new career goals.

- Start by thinking about and writing down your transferrable skills.
- Research the industry and job descriptions that are similar to the position you are seeking.
- Connect with the people on your success team. Ask them for advice and referrals to others you can connect with in your desired occupation or field of interest to learn more about a position or industry.
- To support your learning about a new field, you may need to network and make connections outside your circle to meet and establish new contacts and relationships with professionals in your desired field.
- Make a list of those people you would like to know, because these are the people that need to know you.
- Get the experience you need via training, education, and certifications.

If you are preparing to lead this transition and can keep your day job while you prepare, consider contracting or freelancing on projects to gain experience in your desired field so you can build your portfolio. Look for volunteer opportunities related to the career you want and add that experience to your résumé. Just as important, make sure your finances are in order in case you have to take a lower salary to get a foot in the door, or move at your own expense because your new company doesn't have a relocation program or benefit. You might be willing to make this sacrifice because the new job offers great growth opportunities.

You're heading into new territory to embark upon a new career. Expect to have challenges along your journey, but don't give up on this exciting adventure. The path to your goal may not be a straight line and the timing may not be what you expect. You may encounter hurdles along the way, but be prepared to go around them or jump over them. Stick to your plan in order to make your career transition a smooth one.

....

"The path to your career goals may not be a straight line."

"Go around the hurdles or jump over them."

SHOUT-OUT

"You are never too old to set another goal
or to dream a new dream."

—Les Brown

28

Taking On Leadership Roles

No matter where you are, at every level,
there are opportunities to lead. No one leadership style fits all.

At every level, there are opportunities for us to take on leadership roles and demonstrate our leadership abilities and capabilities. Volunteering or being assigned to take on a project can help develop our leadership skills and gain experience as well as enhancing our visibility for mentors and sponsors looking to identify those with leadership potential.

Be alert for opportunities where you can take on responsibilities that will elevate you and allow you to shine. Note that this often requires you to do more than what is in your current job description but will allow you to demonstrate the knowledge and skills you can offer. Often, these are duties that have been overlooked but can increase the organization's reputation and bottom line.

It is important that you have an understanding beforehand of what is expected of you, what success looks like, what resources will be provided, and who will be responsible for answering any questions that may arise. Also, it is a good idea to develop check-in points with your supervisor to ensure you are on the right track and are kept up to date on any feedback or changes that might occur.

Women, especially women of color, often face a higher level of scrutiny than their counterparts, making visibility a double-edged sword in leadership roles. Studies show that Black and minority women leaders are frequently placed in high-stakes or crisis situations, often referred to as the *glass cliff*, where they are given opportunities to lead but under precarious conditions. Asking questions to gain clarity is always a good idea.

In addition, Black and minority women are often placed in ancillary positions that don't directly impact the bottom line and therefore lack a clear path for advancement. If this sounds like your situation, do all that you can to turn the opportunity to your advantage. These specialized leadership assignments may not have been done before and could give you the chance to offer new ideas along with your skills.

Taking on a leadership role is an opportunity to model resilience and inspire others. Embracing challenging assignments and crisis situations can strengthen credibility and build a track record of success. No matter your level or position, start where you are and build your leadership status one project at a time, creating a strong track record for performance and a reputation for getting the job done. Develop a strong network within and outside the organization. Networks that cross organizational functions can provide new perspectives, support, and resources—all essential for long-term success.

Understanding your strengths also includes understanding your leadership style. If the project you are assigned includes leading a team, think about *how* you are going to lead your team. Are you going to lead by delegating? By telling others what you want them to do? By giving others a say in how they are going to do the work? While there are several leadership styles, the best style of all is to be *agile*. Since no one leadership style fits all organizations or determines how you manage individuals on the same team, you need to know when to switch between different styles based on different circumstances. Knowing which style is *yours* and what styles you need to practice will be key to your leadership success.

Below are a few examples of the leadership styles we talked about in our first book:

Authoritarian (also known as *autocratic*): This leader has total control over employees, makes decisions based on their own ideas, and does not seek input from the team. This is usually the manager that people don't enjoy working with.

Charismatic: This leader uses their natural personality and charm to motivate and inspire to keep team members engaged to achieve organizational goals.

Transactional: This leader is focused on results and relies on a structured approach that includes rewards and reprimands to motivate employees to perform well.

Transformational: This leader inspires the team with intellectual stimulation and a vision of the future that encourages individuals to grow, think outside the box, and exceed performance expectations.

Participative (also known as *democratic*): This leader actively involves team members in the decision-making process, which fosters open communication and collaboration.

Bureaucratic: This leader enforces a hierarchical structure and a clear chain of command, where each level has a clearly defined role, and usually operates by the book with no exceptions.

Delegative (also known as *laissez-faire*): This is a hands-off leadership style where the leader assigns tasks to the team and trusts its members to complete them.

Situational: This leader adapts her approach to the situation and often uses coaching as a developmental tool to help the team achieve organizational goals.

From this list, identify your leadership style, then learn more about the others and practice them. You can adjust the style you need to implement according to who you're leading and the circumstances. Your best leadership style, or the one you're most comfortable with, is usually the one derived from your personality, life and family experiences, emotional intelligence, and way of thinking.

Taking on leadership roles and understanding your leadership style will improve your communication and collaboration skills, increase your problem-solving and strategic thinking skills, and ultimately, raise your visibility within your department and company. Given this, whatever your current role, whenever opportunities for leadership come your way, be ready to take on new responsibilities that can help you gain exposure and grow your career.

SHOUT-OUTS
. . . .

"It's up to you to bring yourself to the attention of powerful people around you. They're not going to find you on their own."

—Richard Parsons

. . . .

"Change will not come if we wait for some other person or some other time. We are the ones we've been waiting for. We are the change that we seek."

—Barack Obama

. . . .

"I suppose leadership at one time meant muscles, but today it means getting along with people."

—attributed to Mahatma Gandhi

29

Work Reentry: How to Onboard Yourself After Time Away

After a layoff, a reorg, or a gap in your work history,
you may have some anxiety over how to get back into the game,
but here are some suggestions to help you prepare for reentry.

When unexpected events impact your career trajectory, you may need to make adjustments and reset before returning to the workplace. Whether you have been fired or laid off, sick or caring for someone who is ill, starting and closing down a business, nurturing a newborn, taking a much-needed mental health break, or whatever your reason, give yourself grace, own your journey, and find your peace.

No one else's experiences are exactly the same as yours, and how you claim your uniqueness in a time of challenge will determine your resilience and can be your superpower. There should be no shame in your circumstances. No Shame! Embrace the moment and welcome the opportunity to evaluate your options and recalibrate your approach.

First and foremost, be sure to support your spirit. This means reflecting, resting, reevaluating, and determining ways to keep upholding yourself as you walk this portion of your journey. Rest as much as you can—your mind, body, and spirit. It is difficult to generate ideas for moving forward when you are exhausted. Even if you think you do not have the time, *stop* and take some time to rest and recuperate anyway.

Reach out to your networks. You may feel uncomfortable, but reach out to those you trust anyway. If some of your connections have broken, repair them and reestablish relationships wherever possible. You may reach out to different people for different reasons—some for support, some for advice, some for written references or recommendations. Of course, some of the strongest members of your networks may be able and willing to help you in as many ways as they can. Be gracious in accepting their assistance, and try not to worry too much about how you can repay them. Chances are that they have been helped by others over the years, and the best way to repay them may be to "pass it forward," and help others as you are able.

It is important to maintain your relationships as much as you can so that you are not reaching out to make an "ask" after a long silence. However, life happens, and there may be exceptions. You may need to seek support from someone whom you do not know at all, or whom you do not know well or have not spoken with in a while. If you are given the opportunity, be frank, open, and honest about why you are communicating with them. Be prepared to receive a "No," or not to receive any response at all. Do your best not to take things personally. Learn all that you can and press ahead.

As you begin to plan for reentry, examine the experiences you have undergone and extrapolate work-related skill development or demonstration so that you can better identify the value you bring back to the workplace. What do you know now that you did not know before your time away? How can this new knowledge benefit you and a potential employer?

Be prepared to share what you have been doing while you were away and what you would like to do next. For example, you may have been handling family matters, church duties, community service work, freelancing, consulting, caregiving, starting and running a business, community organizing, taking a course, learning a new language, pursuing a degree, or something else. In reality, you were probably doing more than one thing, and you can describe those experiences in your career documents (vita, résumé, bio, etc.) and articulate them when you explain any gaps in your formal work experience.

While you should be prepared to address any gaps on your career timeline truthfully and authentically, you do *not* need to apologize or go into too much detail. You can correlate your job and life experiences to the position description and requirements as appropriate.

Before you reach out, you can practice telling your story with friends, former colleagues, career coaches, and others whom you trust so that you can speak about what you have learned or gained from your time away without oversharing or being apologetic or embarrassed. Your journey is valid, and you are not alone, although you may feel that way.

Take advantage of any groups that may offer free or low-cost resources and support as you conduct your search, whether in-person or virtual. Trade organizations, conferences, and online networks within or outside of your industry may serve as lifelines for you as you craft a path back to the workplace. You may want to start your own group if you cannot find one that is right for you.

Career coaches, chambers of commerce, industry organizations, mentors, former colleagues, former managers, sororities, fraternities, churches, online career advisors, books, journals, and podcasts may all provide some guidance for you as you navigate this portion of your journey. However, remember that you are the architect of your career trajectory, and you can design it as you see fit. Remember, you cannot leave all the work to others.

When you are hired, you will want to take advantage of the orientation and training programs for new or returning employees if they are available. You may also want to take additional classes to support your onboarding or "reboarding" program, with special emphasis on new skills you want to develop or skills you want to polish up or refresh.

You can embrace and even learn to cherish the time spent away from your workplace, whether voluntary or involuntarily imposed. After time away, you may decide to find another position in the industry you left, or you may go in an entirely different direction. You do have choices, but doing nothing and waiting to be called is not an option. Whatever you decide to do for reentry, know that you can do it and do it well.

....

"You can get back into the game, and you can win!"

"It may take time to get back in, but keep the faith, it will happen!"

SHOUT-OUT

"In this game, everyone needs a break to refuel, recharge, and jump back in full throttle."

—Helen Edwards

30

Learning from Rejection, Recovering from Disappointment

One door closes and another door opens.
Learn from experiences and bounce back.

Possible scenarios:

- You were up for a promotion that you feel you deserved, but you did not get it.
- Someone less qualified was elevated over you.
- You received a performance appraisal that you feel was unfair or just wrong.
- You believe that you were inaccurately depicted in some way, whether in person, online, or while you were absent.
- You were a candidate for a job that you were sure you would get. You did not.

How can you come back from rejections, putdowns, and disappointments, no matter how they occur or what form they take? We have all had these experiences and survived them. You may have your own scenario to add to this list.

Here are some strategies for living with these circumstances, learning from them, and leaping forward.

First, you must "own" your situation—the reality of it—not just what you surmise or heard happened or believe happened. What actually happened? How can you find out? Who can you vet or check the facts with—trusted present or former colleagues, friends, family members, mentors, or the actual decision-makers? Who will tell you the truth? Once you have ascertained what has happened as best you can, you can begin to sort out your feelings about the situation and then determine what, if anything, you want to do about it.

Next, embrace your feelings. Too often, we have been told that we must *never* let "them" see us sweat, emote, cry, scream, or just be human. You may know of someone who has had a panic attack, hyperventilated, developed an ulcer, suffered migraine headaches, lost her hair, suffered a stroke or a mental breakdown, was hospitalized for depression, drank too much or used drugs, could not sleep, or you or someone you know may have physically or mentally suffered in other ways. One of us has been hospitalized for depression and, through treatment, found healthier approaches to dealing with stress. There is no shame here.

We have to find "safe" spaces and people with whom we can share our feelings when we are discouraged. They may be professionals—therapists, counsellors, psychologists, psychiatrists, or others. They may be friends or family members. Whoever they are, you must give yourself permission to seek them out. Letting your feelings fester can lead to short- or long-term health problems. Tragically, some of us have even lost beautiful and brilliant friends to suicide, perhaps because they felt isolated and were unable to reach out for help.

Contrary to popular (and our own) beliefs, Black women are in fact human beings—not superhuman Wonder Women! As humans, we already have the right to our feelings. We do not have to "earn" them by working so hard that we put ourselves out of commission—killing ourselves for being human. *Just stop!*

Honor your feelings! Talk them out with people you trust or even in front of your own mirror. You can also write out your feelings in a journal, whether in print or online, or you can record your feelings on tape. However you do it, *get them out.*

Then take some time to just be. If you can get away from the day-to-day, do so and give yourself time and permission to relax, reflect, or just do nothing. Whatever you do, don't feel that you must respond quickly and publicly to a disappointment. *Take the time you need.*

Now consider your options. First and foremost, do you need to respond at all? Sometimes, the best response, even to a heartfelt disappointment, is no response at all. This may go against your grain, as we are often programmed to be women of action who immediately take steps to right a wrong. Not acting may be difficult and painful, but it also may be best. Sometimes your silence can be your strongest response.

If you feel you must act, how can you do so and keep your self-respect? There may be a formal action that you can take—filing a complaint, launching an investigation, or otherwise challenging the decision you feel was unfair or discriminatory. Before you take such a formal action, be sure to consult with an attorney or someone with experience on the process and possible outcomes.

You may consider meeting with the decision-maker(s) on your own to more fully understand their reasoning. You can seek reconsideration of their decision, which may be a rare outcome, but it can happen. You might also submit a written response to the decision-makers that sets forth your reasoning and proposes a solution you believe is more fair. This proposal could include the creation of a position for you or a lateral move for you within the organization.

You may be offered a severance package. If so, it may be wise to speak with someone you trust to determine whether there are points you want to negotiate before you decide to take it. You may decide to leave without one. Whatever you decide, take the action that feels right to you and don't look back. You will find that as you take each step forward, the next step(s) will unfold or present themselves.

Find the lesson(s) in your experiences and apply them as you move forward. What have you learned? What else can you learn? How can you pass your lessons forward? Treasure your learnings and life lessons.

Support your spirit and reach out to your community and networks as you learn from your experiences and strike out on your next adventures. Is it time to launch your own business? Is it time to acquire some new skills? Is it time to look for another job? Thinking through your new options can lead to opportunities that you didn't think were possible.

Is it time to do all these things and/or something else? Be open to your next steps. Think. Believe. Consult. Consider. Trust. Then Act.

SHOUT-OUTS

"We fall down, but we get up."

—Donnie McClurkin

. . . .

"The way to win is to try."

—Stacey Abrams

. . . .

"Men's best successes come after their disappointments."

—Henry Ward Beecher

Leading from a Place of Vulnerability

Feeling unsure or uncertain about the path forward—and having the
courage to disclose that uncertainty—does not mean you aren't a good
leader. In fact, it may mean just the opposite.

Many of us have been programmed to believe that exposing our
vulnerability—our humanity—in our workplace can be dam-
aging or detrimental to our ability to lead. Particularly for those of us who
are women of color, we may believe that we must wear our emotional
coat of armor at all times.

Beyond the long-held notion that we should never let them see us
sweat, we have found that most women leaders also believe that we
should never let them see us cry, get angry, or display any uncertainty
or ambivalence when making a decision, even a difficult or complicated
one. This leadership standard is archaic and unrealistic and can stifle
emotionally intelligent and reasoned decision-making. Whether you are
setting strategic goals, planning and managing budgets, or problem-
solving, pausing to consider more than one outcome or even reconsider-
ing your process for arriving at an outcome can lead to a stronger, better
result.

Contrary to our long-held beliefs and practices, it can be liberating
to shed a layer or two of our protective shields as leaders. In our work,
we have found that many leaders (especially women) are concerned that

if they share any hint of uncertainty or dare to say, "I don't know," they run the risk of being perceived as incompetent, indecisive, or emotional. However, as our society and world grow even more complex, it is simply not possible for any leader to know exactly what to do at all times. With so much information available at our fingertips in so many different formats, it can be overwhelming to pick the right data and right resource to make an important decision in an instant.

The reality is that making good decisions often takes time, and as a strong leader, you may need to consider a range of options and explore them fully before making a final determination. Others may try to make you feel inadequate . . . don't let them. Your willingness to openly and thoroughly consider more than one path forward (perhaps including combining ideas to create a new, uncharted path) is a sign of strength. Uncertainty or ambivalence can be perceived as the smart way to review all the possibilities, and sharing your thoughts and feelings can make you seem more human to your team and colleagues.

While it may be risky to step off the podium of "I always know what to do at any given moment," we have found that being honest about your uncertainty and displaying your ability to consider all aspects of a problem—even complex and seemingly contradictory ones—can lead to greater understanding and respect from your team and colleagues. This consideration can result in better and stronger decision-making.

We recommend that you:

- Learn to be more fluid in your decision-making, acting on the best information available at the time, with the understanding that additional data received at a later date could impact prior decisions.
- Sit with your uncertainty. Embrace it. Do not run from it or assume that feeling it makes you "weak." Not so! You are smart and thoughtful. Let your uncertainty guide you to consider creative ways to problem solve.

- Rely on your gut, your faith, your "inner knowing." Do not allow yourself to be rushed into a hasty, poorly thought-out decision. Your moral foundation, seasoned with your wisdom and experience, will not lead you astray.
- Consult your success team, advisors, colleagues, and friends as appropriate. Then listen to your own inner voice and move forward.

....

"It is not a crime to be human."

"Take the risk! You may be the stronger for it."

SHOUT-OUTS

"The great leaders are not the strongest,
they are the ones who are honest about their weakness."

—Simon Sinek

32

Redefining Career Success

What career success looks like for one may be totally different for another. It's okay to change your mind about what you want to do and how far you want to go. Reevaluate your goals to determine what's important to you.

Career success means different things to different people, and how you define it is a personal decision. To one person it may mean starting in an entry-level position in corporate America, climbing the corporate ladder, and becoming a vice president or above, as we have done. To another, it may mean building a business from scratch, becoming an entrepreneur, and then selling the business and starting the process all over again. To yet another, career success could mean working at a job where they don't have to spend a lot of time at work, because they'd rather invest and put in more hours with their family. And someone else may want to work at a nonprofit where they feel that giving and pouring into others is more aligned with their spirit, and provides a sense of accomplishment.

If you haven't done so already, take the time to define what career success truly means to you, and what it looks like to you. Establishing your standards for success is critical to building a career that reflects your own unique goals and is not shaped by society's expectations or someone else's definition of success.

Defining and redefining your career success is up to you. It means evaluating and reevaluating your goals to determine what's important to you at any given point in time—and what's important may change at different stages of your career. Your goals may change depending upon the circumstances throughout your life, your priorities, and changing interests. In other words, how you measure and define success in your fifties is probably different from the way you defined it in your twenties, thirties, and forties.

Besides, not everyone's goal is to wind up in the C-suite. Of course, the higher up you go on the career pyramid, the narrower it gets, with one person or a few people at the top. The higher you climb, the bigger the stakes and the greater the competition, which can sometimes lead to great personal sacrifice.

The traditional career path—earn a degree, secure a good job, stay with a company, and advance—is a paradigm that no longer exists. New technology that requires reskilling and upskilling is changing the way we work. AI is reshaping the workforce, and it's here to stay. We may have to adjust and possibly redefine our career strategies from time to time. In this era of new technology, we are expected to be flexible, learn, adapt, grow, and redefine.

Given this, take the time to determine how you define career success so you can recognize it when you achieve it. For example, write down what financial success in your career looks like to you. Is it based on salary, bonus, promotions, tangible items like owning multiple homes, taking multiple vacations per year? And if you redefine financial success, what will it look like now? Write it down. Consider any new circumstances. You may decide that a second home is no longer a priority because property taxes have increased, or that reaching the next senior level position is no longer important because you just found out you're expecting and now feel the need to spend more time at home.

Then look at your internal measure of success. What determines your sense of happiness and enjoyment at work? For example, after a company reorganization, you may decide you are not happy with your new assignment. You might decide to redefine your career success by seeking a job transfer or a position outside your company where you feel you will have more work fulfillment and satisfaction.

Keep your options open when it comes to defining and redefining career success. Decide what's important to you and establish standards for success that are aligned with your values and career goals. Only you are driving this bus, and only you will determine which route you want to take and the distance you want to travel. How you measure, define, and redefine your success is entirely up to you.

SHOUT-OUTS

"It's about redefining what success is, and what our roles are,
so we can be gentler on ourselves—
and so we can get rid of the G-word [guilt]."

—Tiffany Dufu

. . . .

"How you position yourself is essential to maximizing your success."

—Carla Harris

. . . .

"There's always hurdles. So I just keep moving, just constantly
redefining myself. That's how you stay in the race."

—Isaac Hayes

33

Personal Brand Building to Create and Get What You Want

Reflect, reevaluate, reposition, and reinvent as needed.
Preparing for a new career, changing industries, learning new skills,
or refreshing existing ones can give you a competitive edge. Define
and redefine yourself. Authenticity is key.

The three simple questions you must ask yourself when you are creating and building your personal brand are:

How do I want others to see me?
What makes me unique?
What do I want to be known for?

You must first decide, based on your values, skills, personality, and experiences, what you want to be known for and how you want the world to see you. Be intentional and authentic in your description of yourself. Creating a personal brand is not about modifying, altering, or embellishing your identity; it's about being genuine and having the self-awareness to present the best of what you have to offer, so others can get to know you and what you stand for and clearly understand your area of expertise.

Decide what makes you unique and distinguishes you from the competition, your co-workers, or others. For example, although your skills and goals may be similar to others', your experiences and approach to executing projects or your communication and leadership styles may differ, which will make your personal brand unique. Your personal brand statement belongs to you. It is a product you can bring up in conversation or market on social media platforms or website, in your résumé, or in your bio.

A personal brand statement can be one to three sentences. Below are some examples:

- Selling is in my DNA, and helping customers solve problems is my passion. I'm committed to every product and project that I take on.
- I help companies streamline their workflow processes so they can be more efficient and effective, and increase profits and productivity.
- I'm a multihyphenate Emmy Award–winning writer, expert at public speaking and leading creative teams.
- My specialty is working with seniors and older adults to help them transition into the world of technology, because I am compassionate, an active listener, aware of their various needs, and I enjoy them very much!
- I'm a passionate corporate leader who helps Black women unlock their full potential to navigate through challenges at work and achieve their business goals via individual coaching and personalized development strategy plans.
- I'm a rock-star storyteller and content creator at the forefront of the digital evolution, creating compelling brand strategies for social media influencers to target multicultural audiences and increase engagement and retention.

A personal brand statement summarizes your personal mission or vision and is aimed at your target audience. Personal branding is meant to leave a first impression to help you stand out, make you memorable, and establish your reputation. If you don't have a personal brand statement, it's important to begin crafting one *today*. Write down your skills, your experiences, your goals, and what's unique about you. This glimpse or snapshot of who you are allows you to create your own narrative, as opposed to leaving it to others. Start by writing a few statements about yourself, and continue to tweak until you're satisfied with one that feels like it's tailor-made.

"So, tell me about yourself" is an opportunity for you to respond with your personal brand, sharing stories about yourself and your experiences. Whether you're at a networking event, informal gathering, or party, in an introductory meeting with a client or customer, at a job interview, or seeking a promotion, your personal brand statement should clearly capture the attention of potential clients, customers, and employers so they can recognize your value as quickly as possible.

Most importantly, your personal brand statement is about *you*. It's to help you get clarity around who you are and how you want to present yourself.

The good news is, your personal brand statement is malleable and not set in stone. You can reevaluate, reframe, reposition, and reinvent as your life and your career goals change. You are the only one who can define and redefine yourself, and each iteration of your brand is an opportunity to strategize to achieve your goals.

We recommend you audit and edit your personal brand statement yearly, or as needed, to make sure it aligns with your goals, fits into your current position, and addresses your changing narrative. Your personal brand statement allows you to better control your professional and personal image, elevate your visibility, and increase your confidence, and provides you with focus and direction. It's your launching pad, and just one tool essential to your success.

. . . .

"Tell your own story before other people
get a chance to tell their stories about you."

"You are the potter who molds the clay
to shape and define your personal brand."

SHOUT-OUT
. . . .

"Your brand is what people say about you
when you're not in the room."

—Jeff Bezos

34

Nothing Stays the Same;
Change Is Inevitable

*Being prepared and ready for change
only puts you ahead of the game.*

Whether you are already in a leadership role or aspiring to attain one, you need to be prepared for both expected and unanticipated shifts in your career and life plans that could occur at any time. We have experienced a number of changes throughout our careers and have learned that our mindset or attitude about what is happening is the key to how we manage these changes successfully.

These changes might look like setbacks: layoffs, demotions, shortened hours, limits on your job duties or the range of your responsibilities, a department shutdown, your company closing, or something else. Other changes might appear as opportunities—a promotion to fill the position of a manager who has retired or resigned, a chance to inaugurate a new position within a longstanding organization, an invitation to join a startup, the launch of your own business, or something else.

Whether the actual changes are within your control or not, how you approach them is always within your control. Although you might feel uncertain or shaky when facing a sudden shift in your career or circumstances, you can still be strategic in making your plans to move forward.

Here are some guidelines for how to be ready to weather the inevitable challenges you are likely to face along your career path.

First and foremost, be ready and stay ready for change, which is the only constant in career planning. Here are some questions to pose to yourself about your "readiness":

- Am I practicing readiness within my spirit and in my life so that I can welcome the changes that are sure to come?
- Am I open to retooling my current skill sets and learning new ones?
- Have I taken advantage of the opportunity for training and coaching at my current job, if they are available?
- Are there free or low-cost courses and/or certifications available online or from other sources (professional organizations, academic institutions, or trade groups) that I could pursue to help me prepare for my next career steps?
- Have I volunteered to do something new or unexplored at my current post that could hone my skills?
- Have I maintained relationships with members of my professional networks and circles of friends (my success teams) so that I feel comfortable consulting them for advice as I plan for my future?

As workplace venues and protocols continue to evolve, here are some questions you can ask yourself about *work cultures*:

- If I have been working remotely or in a hybrid setting, how can I educate myself on the new protocols and rules of etiquette pertaining to my return to the physical workplace? Can present or former colleagues assist me? Can family members or friends with diverse work histories give me some pointers?

- Can I collaborate with other new or returning leaders and co-workers so that we can help one another?
- In addition to whatever may be written about my organization or industry—about our mission and workforce rules—can sponsors, mentors, or other experts help me prepare to be a valuable addition to my new team, whatever my role will be?

Our own experiences and our work with longtime and emerging leaders have taught us that we must all become a lot more comfortable with being uncomfortable—stepping far outside our comfort zones. Changes in our careers often appear as challenges, and we must learn to embrace them and meet them directly.

Here are some queries for you about *Dis-Comfort*:

- Am I willing to step outside of my usual behaviors and reactions and take on new attitudes as I assume additional or novel responsibilities?
- Do I have someone to speak with (sponsor, mentor, friend, or career coach) who can help me to get out of my own way and take steps to activate a new vision of myself and my capabilities?
- Can I give myself grace as I ponder and plan to take a leap into a role I had not anticipated?
- How can I learn from this new opportunity so that I can apply the lessons from this experience to my next moves?

You may be surprised by how ready you are to weather the winds of change throughout your career—maybe more ready than you think. All our prior experiences, in our life and in our work, help us to transform any unexpected setback into a move on a chessboard so that we can think about it, consult with others, and then decide upon our next move. Strategically.

We have learned that when you are seeking or creating a position, it can help to focus on what is needed by the clients, customers, and community being served, and to think beyond any specific statement of requirements on a job description. Be able to state how you, with your skills and experience, can address the needs of the audience to be served. How can you enhance or expand the services being provided?

The leaders and aspiring leaders who can efficiently share their abilities and demonstrated excellence in addressing the needs that must be met are more likely to navigate the changes along their career trajectories smoothly and successfully. Like them, you can be ready, stay ready, sound ready, and even look ready for advancement.

Learn to think more broadly about yourself and your possibilities. Be willing to search for and take on opportunities that may not look like the traditional ones. You may make a lateral move to a job similar to the one you have that offers a better chance for promotion. You might enter an entirely new field and work your way up from the ground floor. You may launch or co-launch an enterprise. You may dream of doing much more.

You must not let your own self-expectations or the expectations of others dictate any limits on what you can achieve. Shoot for the stars!

SHOUT-OUTS
....

"Not everything that is faced can be changed,
but nothing can be changed until it is faced."

—James Baldwin

....

"The changes we dread most may contain our salvation."

—Barbara Kingsolver

....

"If anyone wants to keep creating they have to be about change."

—Miles Davis

35

Authenticity: To Be or Not to Be Yourself

There are no hard-and-fast, right or wrong rules about authenticity in the workplace, but where you feel the happiest—most comfortable, motivated, and supported—is likely where you'll be the most successful.

Whenever we have a speaking engagement, there is always someone in the audience who asks us about authenticity: whether or not we, as Black women, can be authentic at work or if we have to be "fake" and misrepresent who we really are. Our answers are usually yes and no and it depends. It depends upon the situation—your role, your company culture—on how you feel, how comfortable you are, and what you believe in. Simply put, it depends upon you and your willingness to adjust under the circumstances.

Authenticity is a state of mind that addresses: *Can I be who I am inside a different culture?* It is generally described as being true to oneself and expressing genuine thoughts, feelings, and actions. However, when at work, you have to strike a balance between being yourself and adapting to the professional environment and company. Ask yourself, *Does the company culture make me feel comfortable? Does the culture accept me for who I am?* Obviously, you don't have to prove that you're Black, but you want to be sure that your work environment is safe enough for you to share the aspects of your culture you feel comfortable exposing.

Authentic interactions can foster stronger relationships and encourage open dialogue about race and identity. These conversations can help build understanding and trust and serve as teachable moments. If, on the other hand, you feel shut down, disregarded, or dismissed by others because of who you are, then perhaps your current workplace is not for you. You want to be in an environment where you can comfortably add value, contribute innovative ideas, be supported and recognized for your talent, work, and leadership responsibilities and capabilities—a place where you can thrive and flourish.

Questions around hair and authenticity also come up in our speaking engagements: natural hair versus straight hair versus sister locs, weaves, and wigs. Hair politics can still be an issue in the workplace. Racial hair discrimination is real. According to research studies around the group of state laws called the CROWN Acts, some women have been fired for wearing natural hair and cultural styles.* Some have not been hired for these same reasons. Others have not been promoted because of their natural hair. The authenticity question around our hair is tricky. If you feel your hairstyle is preventing you from achieving leadership success, you may want to consider a different style, or come to terms with the fact it's time to move on.

CROWN stands for Create Respectful and Open World for Natural hair. The first CROWN Act was introduced in 2019 by Dove and the CROWN Coalition, in partnership with then state senator Holly J. Mitchell of California to ensure protection against discrimination based on race-based hairstyles such as braids, locs, twists, and knots in the workplace and public schools. To bring awareness to the issue, Dove and LinkedIn co-commissioned the 2023 Crown Workplace Research Study to deal with the systemic impact of hair bias and discrimination. A few highlights: (1) the study found that 54 percent of Black women are likely to feel they have to wear their hair straight for a job interview. (2) Nearly half of all Black women under the age of thirty-four feel pressured to have a professional headshot with straight hair. (3) Over 20 percent of Black women

---

* www.thecrownact.com

ages twenty-five to thirty-four have been sent home from work because of their hair.

Historically, we've had to modify our hairstyles to fit into the workplace. In some parts of the country, and in some industries, this is still the case. We all know that, while chemical relaxers, hot combs, and blowouts have made our hair straight, these things have damaged it as well, causing alopecia, thinning hair, and hair loss. Thank goodness it's becoming more acceptable to wear protective styles. In fact, today's wigs are so natural that it's hard to tell if the hair is coming from your scalp or a cap.

Even though workplaces are becoming more accepting of natural hair, straight hair is still associated with being more professional. Likewise, leadership is associated with being more "professional." So it's up to you to decide, based on your beliefs, what is authentic for you and what is not. We know women who wear conservative wigs to work and, when they get home, toss the wigs and flaunt the beautiful bantu knots or twists underneath. Remember our chapter titled "Acknowledge There Is a Game and Accept That You Must Play"? Think about it.

We've also encountered a woman who changed her hairstyle practically every other day with color, various wigs, and sew-ins until it became a challenge, to the point of distraction, for her co-workers to even recognize her on a daily basis. As a leader, you definitely don't want to be perceived as a distraction and not be taken seriously.

The benefits of diversity and inclusion are to provide different perspectives and points of view. The strength of an organization is its ability to find new solutions, come up with innovative ways to drive and increase revenue, and engage staffing that reflects its customers and clients. If you're not in a place where you feel you can be authentic, you're probably not going to be motivated to maximize your leadership potential or be recognized for it.

At the end of the day, you just want to be considered for the same opportunities as everyone else. Not being yourself can invite a whole host of other problems, like feelings of inadequacy, emotional stress, low self-esteem, and a variety of physical ailments such as stomach ulcers, hives, and hair loss. You can't let that happen to you.

Duality and code-switching also play a role in authenticity (see chapter 6). These are tools that can help us be successful in every part of our lives. It's almost like changing leadership styles—knowing which style is best to use in any particular situation. You wouldn't show up to a black-tie event in a pair of jeans. Authenticity is about being self-aware and knowing what is best to help you achieve your goals. Ultimately, wherever you are, whatever role you're in, you'll be happier and more successful being yourself.

....

"Authentic leaders are trusted leaders."

SHOUT-OUTS

"Authenticity is the daily practice of letting go of who we think we're supposed to be and embracing who we are."

—Brené Brown

....

"When you bring your authentic self to the table, people will trust you. And trust is the heart of any successful relationship."

—Carla Harris

36

Acknowledging, Embracing, and Leveraging Your Personal Power

You already have the power you think you need
to acquire from others. Here's how to cultivate it.

As women, we may not be aware of the personal power and presence we already have. We may assume, as a result of the many subtle and overt messages we receive as girls and young women in our society, that we are only as powerful as the positions we hold, the ones we seek, or the partners, mates, spouses, lovers we have chosen or who have chosen us. We may think that our friends, sorority sisters, classmates, colleagues, and the connections we have developed over time give us our power. We may believe that it is our assets, holdings, properties, or even our locations (where we live, etc.) that bring us power. We may think our power comes from our surroundings rather than from within. All too often, our society and much of our world seem to signal that we women are powerful because of what we *do* or who we *know* instead of who we *are*. Not so.

We believe that your personal power originates within you, and it has little to do with and cannot be limited by the external indicators of your success or perceived lack of it. Your power lies within you. It is your personal light, and you should not let anyone extinguish it.

First and foremost, you must believe in yourself. You must. Whether you are faith-based or not, you must get in touch with your inner self, connect with your personal foundation of principles, morals, and beliefs, and honor it. This inner strength is where your real power lies.

As you become more comfortable with your authentic self and identify what makes you unique, you can recognize and embrace the power that arises out of your being you. You are your own superpower. You are a supernova waiting to be discovered . . . by you!

Many of us have spent years trying to be the person we felt we should be, without ever really exploring our visions for ourselves and our own lives. We owe it to "us" to find out who we really are and strengthen our inner cores.

While some of us may seek counselling from professionals, others of us have found that daily or regular journaling can be helpful. Participating in group work at retreats or in workshops can help us discover or uncover our deepest desires for ourselves and identify our skill sets as leaders. We may set off on solo sojourns to learn how to listen to that "still, small voice" that gives us the guidance we need when facing life's challenges.

As we reflect and learn more about ourselves and believe in our own possibilities, we can unleash our personal power and potential—unconstrained by what we may have heard from others—and create a vision for ourselves. Although it may be helpful to observe ways that others wield their power, remember that you can determine your own strategies to use the power you already hold and then build upon them.

You can practice your powerfulness by thinking, speaking, and acting with intention and purpose. Be mindful about how and whether you choose to engage with others or respond to challenging situations. Test how you feel when you take certain actions or choose not to act. As you make peace with your inner feelings, your sense of power will increase, and you will rely more on your own inner compass.

You can practice exerting your power with others whom you trust or just look in the mirror and try out more powerful ways of speaking. Remember to believe in yourself!

As we have written, the first person you lead is *you*. So, it stands to reason that you must learn to empower yourself and activate your leadership potential. Whether you embark on your own solitary sojourn to personal empowerment, work with others to grow your power, or some combination of these two approaches, once you have tapped into your well of personal power, you will find your own voice and become unstoppable: resilient, courageous, persistent, and emboldened.

. . . .

"You've got the power. Use it!"

SHOUT-OUTS

"The most common way people give up their power
is by thinking they don't have any."

—commonly attributed to Alice Walker

. . . .

"Our deepest fear is not that we are inadequate.
Our deepest fear is that we are powerful beyond measure."

—Marianne Williamson

37

Making Big, Bold Moves
at the Height of Your Career

You've reached the top. Now what? Brace yourself for something new.
No need to feel stuck. Consider moving for opportunity: promotion,
changing industries, and relocation are all options.

One thing we know for sure: our world needs more women in leadership roles in more fields. Everywhere. We are seeing women leaders take risks to manage in more inclusive and compassionate ways. This is both progressive and necessary. Too often we have coached women executives who are worn out from stewarding so many others in their lives and putting their own dreams aside.

We know that women throughout history have risen to serve their communities and their nations, but all too often their contributions have been obscured, falsified, or buried, often with others taking the credit for their ideas, inventions, artistic creations, and policies. Thanks to the work of historians, scholars, librarians, museum curators, and others, we can more easily access accurate information about the myriad ways women have helped to make our world better.

Still, many of us have been advised not to take too many risks as we advance in our careers—not to be too loud, too adventurous, or too big, because we would be perceived as "too much." Too much for whom? Certainly not for us.

We have had to multitask all our lives, and we are not afraid to welcome those who may not look, think, or sound like us. Our ability to lead across differences is sorely needed, especially now. We believe that women bring a certain *je ne sais quois* to leadership—an ability to see clearly and lead compassionately. Women can accommodate and incorporate diverse points of view and approaches to problem-solving without being intimidated by the different strengths of others.

Although you may want to stretch your wings, others may feel that you have reached a well-earned plateau and should perch there for a while and take advantage of the perks and benefits of your hard-won post. And so you should, if you really want to do this.

Many of us have parents and other guardians as role models, working hard and sacrificing much to get and keep good jobs. They laid the foundation for us to have opportunities that they did not so we could pursue our career goals, giving us roots and wings for which we are grateful. While we have strengthened our roots and used what we have learned to help others, perhaps it is time to dust off our dreams, spread our wings, and make our own big, bold moves!

We know how scary it can be to leave the known (even if we are sick of it) and pursue the unknown, but we have to take risks if we really want to move in new directions. Sometimes we try to talk ourselves out of making our next moves by listing all the things we don't know or cannot predict about the new opportunity, including our lack of experience in a specific arena. We can really get in our own way.

Take the chance. Learn what you can. Talk with someone who has taken a leap, even if they are doing something outside of your areas of interest. We have found that their courage, optimism, war stories, and energy can spur our own.

Is there something you have longed to do or try but have not because you felt it was not safe? Now is the time to expand your boundaries and reach for a new tier, preferably one of your own making.

Perhaps you want to live and work abroad. With our ever-advancing technologies, you can. Would you like to join with friends and family to launch a business venture, community initiative, or church project? That sense of adventure—of breaking new ground—is exactly how this book (and our earlier two books) got written and our company started. Get to it!

You can also make a big move or career change entirely on your own. We recommend that you gather as much information as you can first. You may want to use your success team as your board of advisors so you can benefit from their wisdom, experience, and support.

Why move now? you may ask. We would ask, why *not* now? You have worked hard and proved yourself to be a strong leader and an effective manager. You have made compromises and set some of your dreams for yourself aside. Pick them back up! The time is now. You won't regret it.

What if it doesn't work out? The truth is that it may not. But according to the great South African world leader and statesman Nelson Mandela, you cannot lose. He has reportedly said, you can only "win or learn."

At the height of your career, whatever you decide to do, you will grow through your experiences and expand your skill sets. You may decide to take even more risks to build the life and career that you love. We hope you will.

. . . .

"Make your move!"

SHOUT-OUTS

"Don't be afraid to take risks,
because that's where growth and opportunity lie."

—Ursula Burns

. . . .

"Am I good enough? Yes, I am."

—Michelle Obama

38

So You're Over Fifty; It Ain't Over Yet

Get over the hump and triumph!

It wasn't long ago that people thought being over fifty meant you were "over the hill." But now we're living longer, healthier lives, have more energy, are more physically active than previous generations, and most importantly, many of us *want* to continue working past fifty and beyond. We don't see retirement as an opportunity to slow down, rest on our laurels, throw in the towel, sit in a rocking chair, and watch the sun set. Rather we see it as a chance to start a new chapter, to keep on working, pick up new skills, learn new technologies, go back to school, become an entrepreneur, consultant, independent contractor—in general, to start anew and flourish. Whatever you do, it's important to be active. These days, age is just a number.

According to studies cited in *Harvard Business Review*, today, 27 percent of Americans ages sixty-five to seventy-four work or are actively looking for jobs. It is projected that by 2032, one in four U.S. workers will be fifty-five or older, and close to one out of every ten will be sixty-five or older. In fact, employees sixty-five or older now represent the fastest growing segment of the workforce.[*]

---

[*] Ken Dychtwald, Robert Morison, and Katy Terveer, "Redesigning Retirement," *Harvard Business Review,* March/April 2024, 73.

So there is no need to slow down if you don't want to. It may be time to rev things up for a third, fourth, or fifth act. Being over fifty translates to a new beginning, doing what you've always wanted to do, and, if you like, turning your passion and hobby into dollars.

Don't let ageism discourage you from pursuing your dream or your goals. If you still want to work, you can prepare for this next stage of your career. As women over fifty, we are seasoned with valuable experience, expertise, strengths, and assets that not only benefit a company but can also foster the development of younger workers. If you've worked at a company or in a corporate space, you also have experience with organizational knowledge, established relationships, and a track record with customers and clients. Plus, you're at an age where you tend to be more loyal and committed to your employer, perhaps, than your younger counterparts. And the best part of being in this next stage of your career is, you don't have to limit yourself to roles you've had in the past. Be open to new jobs, opportunities, and responsibilities. If you encounter feedback like "You're overqualified for this position," frame your response to focus on all the benefits your experience brings to the company, the department, and the team. Let the interviewer know how you can support the success of your boss, even if that person is younger than you.

There are several job sites that specialize in providing opportunities for older workers, in addition to other sources—books, webinars, online courses, and organizations—that can help you map out your future. The truth is, it may take corporations a while to recognize all the advantages of retaining older workers—the many ways they can keep utilizing us and keep us engaged with new training, lateral moves, new teams, project work, and new responsibilities. Start laying the groundwork for what's next for you now, because it ain't over, no matter your age. As you enter this next stage of your career, you have more freedom, and your best days could well be ahead of you rather than behind you.

If your dream is to turn your passion, hobby, or talents into a role as an entrepreneur, independent contractor, or consultant, it's best to prepare a strategy and action plan while you're still on the job. If you haven't begun the process while at work, don't worry, you can begin when you leave your position. There are many resources available to guide you through the process of running your own business. To maximize your success, it's critical to keep your skills fresh, maintain your networks, re-connect with former colleagues, and establish new relationships as you embark upon this new season of your life.

Over fifty has now become synonymous with "your time": a time for you to redefine, re-create, reinvent, and reposition a new you. You've worked hard to get here and are blessed to be here, so dig deep into your ambition and find a new or different way to continue to fulfill your purpose. Now, that's something to look forward to.

SHOUT-OUTS

"Age is no issue to me. Fifty is the new thirty.
Seventy is the new fifty. There are no rules that say
you have to dress a certain way, or be a certain way."

—Tina Turner

. . . .

"You're never too old to chase your dream."

—Diana Nyad

. . . .

"Never be limited by other people's limited imaginations."

—Dr. Mae Jemison

39

Steps to Take Before Launching Your Own Business

Stepping out on your own?
Here's what you need to know before becoming an entrepreneur.

You may have thought about launching your own business for several years, or you may have only recently decided to step outside your comfort zone to become your own boss. However you entered the starting gate, you are in good company.

Small business owners have flourished in the economy, serving as revenue generators, key employers, and community builders. Over the past several years, the number of Black women–owned enterprises has grown exponentially, and all indicators point to even more of these businesses in the future.

Here are some questions to ask yourself and six steps we believe will help you prepare to become a successful business owner:

1. **Know your purpose.** Why do you want to start your business? What needs will you be serving in your community? Who is your customer, and how well do you know them? Are you addressing a long-standing need in a new, unique way? Are you passionate about what you will be doing and committed for the long term?

Are you sure you want to do this? Know your *why* before you hang out your shingle or put up your signs—whether virtual or actual.

2. **Do your homework!** Do you have the skill sets you need to start and run your business? Are there others with businesses like the one you have in mind in your area or community? If so, are they likely to be competitors or collaborators? Are there retired business executives who can give you guidance (such as SCORE)*? Are there other resources you can tap into at no or low cost to help you get ready? Are there courses you can take to shore up your knowledge? Are there organizations you already belong to or can join (chambers of commerce, trade or industry groups, professional networks, sororities or fraternities, community centers, etc.) or consultants you can contact who specialize in new-business incubation and support? Do you have friends who have become business owners who would be willing to help you? Note that community colleges, universities, and even local governments may offer classes and certifications that are helpful. Be sure to search out data to make sure there is an audience/clientele for your particular products and/or services.

3. **Draft your business plan.** What do you hope to achieve, and by when? What are your short- and long-term goals? What resources will you need, and what have you already gathered? Are you planning to be an independent owner or are you willing to consider a partnership or a collective? Do you need a brick-and-mortar space or can you launch and operate your business virtually? There are many examples of competent business plans available online. There are also competitions run by business organizations and governments that invite potential business owners to submit their business plans for review and funding.

---

*   www.score.org

4 **Establish and build your brand.** While your business plan should set out the details of your campaign to design and launch your company, it is vital that you also have a brand that clearly presents you and your mission. You may need a logo of your own, a website, and social media marketing plan that precede the launch (whether soft or more formal) of your business. While you can use available technology to accomplish much of your brand building yourself, it may be worth your while to hire an expert to assist you. Your brand should answer these questions: Who are you and what do you stand for? Why should clients trust you and your products or services? How will customers be helped by your company? Do you have any useful references to list on your website or elsewhere (with their permission, of course) that reflect the benefits of your products and services?

5. **Get your money straight!** In addition to the business-plan competitions that often include funding grants as a prize for the top plans submitted, there are small business loans that may be available from financial institutions and government agencies in your area. You are to be congratulated if you have savings that can secure the start of your business and keep you afloat for the first few years. Make plans to cover your expenses in case it takes longer than expected to generate a profit. You can certainly consider partnerships or investors (including but not limited to family members) to be sure that you have the resources you need.

6. **Experts can help.** In addition to the resources, people, and institutions we have already listed, you may need to consult attorneys, accountants, and technology experts. Be sure to secure the name and identity of your enterprise with copyright and trademark filings and protections. Your state may also require certain compliance documents and filings, as well as the designation of an agent. You will need to be sure of your tax status and requirements. You also need to take steps to secure the

privacy of your company's data and any information collected from your clients that you have stored. Even if you operate as a sole owner, you may want to create an advisory board to support you as you build out your business. Particularly if you need product development and distribution expertise, your success team / board of advisors can provide helpful guidance.

Above all, you need to be sure that you are emotionally ready for the excitement, thrilling challenges, and devastating disappointments associated with starting and maintaining your own business. Despite your best long-range planning, unforeseen challenges may occur—a natural disaster, a pandemic, a distribution disruption, your own illness, or the loss of someone in your family or on your team, etc. You must be ready for anything and determined to proceed no matter what happens. If you can maintain your passion for and commitment to your business despite all else, you will succeed.

....

"Plan your work and work your plan."

"Step by step leads to success!"

"Be your own boss! You won't regret it."

SHOUT-OUT

"Success is the result of perfection, hard work, learning from failure, loyalty, and persistence."

—Colin Powell

40

Pass the Baton to the Next Generation

When given the opportunity, help someone take the next step or make a valued connection. We need to support one another and help prepare the next generation. No more crabs in the barrel.

In the spirit of the griots, the messengers of oral tradition of West African culture who were revered as leaders and advisors, who passed down stories from generation to generation, and traveled from village to village and city to city, our goal is to share our stories and what we know about leadership as living wisdom as we travel, and to spread the word, reach back and bring others along. Nowadays, since more of us are choosing to stay in the workforce, we also see a need to reach sideways to peers to bring them along, so that we can continue to help as many women as possible achieve their leadership goals. Griots, aunties, sister friends, sisters, leadership experts, advisors—however you'd like to refer to us, however you may think of us—we are all in this village together.

Reaching back can be done in many ways. Mentoring is time well spent, regardless of age. You can reach back and bring others along by sharing information and providing valuable feedback. Since we don't always get honest feedback from our bosses or others, we can listen to stories and share strategies for solutions that offer different perspectives. We can provide guidance and leads to new jobs or volunteer projects that will help open doors to opportunities. We can share experiences and contacts, and make introductions to and for others. We can also invite individuals to join us at organizational and professional meetings and events, so they can learn new skills, meet new people, and potentially start to build or expand their own networks and success teams.

The point is, no more "I've got mine, now you get yours" way of thinking. No more sabotaging ourselves or, worse, one another. Many of us have strong egos and personalities, but we shouldn't let our power struggles get in the way of achieving the common goal. As our mamas used to say, there's enough in this world for everyone. The need to reach back and support one another is greater now than ever before.

A recent report by the Washington Area Women's Foundation finds "a trend: the pushing out of Black women in leadership."* In both public and private sectors, Black women are finding themselves in unsupportive work environments, doing their best to manage overwhelming or unrealistic workloads. You may have had this experience yourself or know of someone who fits this description. As many of us continue to shatter the "glass ceiling," we may now find ourselves on what researchers call a *glass cliff*—a phenomenon where Black women are elevated into senior leadership roles with the expectation that they will address organizational deficiencies without company support, budgets, staff, or the resources needed to be successful. The study also finds that as the result of these unfair work conditions, some Black women are choosing to leave their jobs altogether.

Because we don't always get what we need within corporate infrastructures, it's imperative that we support ourselves with community and create our own village. None of us has gotten to where we are in a vacuum. We all stand on the shoulders of others who have come before us, with each generation passing the baton and supporting the next. We must continue this tradition. Even if it sometimes appears that the pendulum is

---

* Cyndi Suarez, "The State of Black Women Leadership Is in Danger," *Nonprofit Quarterly*, November 28, 2023.

swinging back, we must be determined to look straight ahead and keep moving forward.

As we step down and retire or rewire, we gladly pass the baton to the young people who are next. We understand and accept that the younger generations work differently than we do. Since they have grown up with technology, require work-life balance, and now have to manage working in a world with AI, a traditional way of working may not be best for them. However, one thing is certain: the laws of leadership are universal, and teams, companies, organizations, and corporations still need to be led. Our families and children still need to be led, and we still need to lead ourselves. Leaders are created, they are not just born, and leadership is here to stay. Despite the world of work changing, leadership is a constant, and, like griots, we will continue to share our stories from village to village and city to city. So rest assured, there ain't no stopping us now, and we ain't gonna let nobody turn us around, which is why each of us must reach back and bring others along.

SHOUT-OUTS

"When Black women win victories,
it is a boost for virtually every segment of society."

—Angela Davis

....

"If you want to lift yourself up, lift up someone else."

—commonly attributed to Booker T. Washington

....

"The way to achieve your own success is
to be willing to help somebody else get it first."

—Iyanla Vanzant

ACKNOWLEDGMENTS

We would like to collectively thank our wonderful and groundbreaking editor at Penguin Random House, Porscha Burke, who has believed in the three of us from the very beginning of our journey together as friends, business partners, and authors. She has grown in leadership experience, wisdom, and grace before our very eyes. She is our guiding light.

We would like to thank our fabulous agent, Cherise Fisher, who has enlightened us and expanded our vision of what an agent actually is and does. We treasure our partnership with her. She is our enthusiastic and effective advocate. We are also thankful for the support of Gerri Warren-Merrick, who continues to be our biggest fan from the original Girls Night Out group.

Lastly, we want to thank the thousands of readers who have lifted us up and supported our work over the years. You have followed us on social media, attended our webinars, spread the word about our books and businesses to your networks, invited us to speak to your organizations, and shared your personal testimonies about how our books and strategies have helped you to navigate your own leadership pathways successfully. You have gifted our books to others and they have gifted them to others as well. You are our family, and we send you blessings.

Many of you have asked us, "What comes next? What is the future of leadership in these trying times?" This book is our answer.

FROM ELAINE

I'd like to thank my mom and dad, Ethele and Elmo Brown, for setting examples of leadership for me to follow and for instilling in me that all things are possible once you put your mind to something. I'd like to thank the many people who believed in me and first helped launch my writing career: Rosemary Bray, Audrey Edwards, Toni Fay, Victoria Sanders, Melody Guy, and Porscha Burke, and to those in my HBO and Time Warner families who celebrated me at the start of this journey. I'm also grateful to my sister, Erica Oliver, who has always been my cheerleader; my son, David; my niece and nephew, Madison and Brendan—all of whom are still growing into the leaders they are destined to be. Also, thank you to my besties, Lynette Hoffler and Joyce Coleman-Sampson, for always being there to lift and support. Last but not least, I'd like to acknowledge NAMIC (National Association for Multi-ethnicity in Communications) for teaching me that leaders aren't just born but that they can be made.

FROM MARSHA

I'd like to thank my mom, Elverso Hook, who was one of the smartest people I knew. She instilled in me the belief that I could succeed at anything that I set my mind and energy toward. I also want to thank my big sister, Shirley Drayton, for always encouraging me and continuing to do so. Thank you to my sons, Shawn, Hart, and Kenny, for keeping me sharp and on my toes. I also must thank my daughter-in-law, Jeantique Bullock, who tries to keep me organized. She is smart, talented, and has a great sense of humor.

A special thanks to Vivian Briggs, whom I have counted on and who has been there for me during a difficult year; Monique Clarke, who is my good friend and technical lifesaver; and Valerie Rainford, who is one of my oldest and dearest friends, who checks in on me and helps me with anything I need. Also, big thanks to Simone Peterson, who is a social media wiz and who keeps me active online, and to Dr. Judith Briles, who continues to share her publishing and marketing expertise with the group of us on a weekly basis.

Last but not least, I am grateful to have had my husband of forty years and my biggest cheerleader, Donald Haygood, to guide and encourage me until his passing earlier this year.

FROM RHONDA
. . . .

I am still standing on the shoulders of my ancestors—including my three grandmothers, Eva, Madeline, and Cora (two by blood and all from love)—who shared their strength, spice, and grace with me throughout my life. Now, with a heavy heart, I must add my beloved husband, Bill; my darling daughter, Kelli; and my remarkable parents, John and Georgianna McLean, to those who have gone ahead to light my way. I am ever grateful to my family members and friends who have stood by me and helped me to move forward.

ABOUT THE AUTHORS

As a writer and producer, Elaine Meryl Brown has made a significant impact in the media and entertainment industry. A former vice president in Creative Services at HBO, her award-winning portfolio showcases a prestigious corporate Emmy Award and over forty industry awards. Her wide array of writing accomplishments include a Daytime Emmy Award for writing ABC-TV's *FYI;* two novels published by Penguin Random House; her status as an Amazon best-selling author on leadership; and several articles published in *Essence* magazine. She is a graduate of NAMIC's Executive Leadership Development Program, the CTAM Executive Management Program at Harvard Business School, as well as the Time Warner Leadership Breakthrough Program at the Simmons University School of Management. She is a member of New York Women in Film & Television, Women's Media Group, and the Producers Guild of America. She has earned an MFA in Creative Writing from Reinhardt University in Waleska, Georgia, and is in the process of writing her third novel, a historical-fiction fantasy.

Marsha Haygood is a keynote speaker, leadership consultant, and talent development strategist. She is a trusted advisor to organizations and leaders who are navigating change, managing talent, and striving to build inclusive, high-performing cultures. With decades of experience in corporate leadership, human resources, and executive development, she equips individuals and teams with the mindset, tools, and strategies needed to lead with purpose and deliver results.

As the founder of StepWise Associates, LLC and co-founder of Black Women of Influence, Marsha has guided senior executives, managers, and rising talent alike, delivering tailored leadership development experiences, engaging workshops, and strategic consulting services for companies seeking to invest in their employees and enhance their workplace culture.

Whether she's training emerging leaders, consulting with organizations on employee engagement and retention, or delivering a keynote that energizes a room, Marsha's mission is consistent: to empower others to lead boldly and move forward with intention. She also continues to offer limited individual and group coaching to professionals ready to level up.

Marsha has been recognized by *The Network Journal* as one of their "Influential Women in Business," and has been honored by the YMCA, The National Association of African Americans in Human Resources, and other organizations for her service and leadership. She has also been featured in a number of publications, including *USA Today, The Daily News, Essence, EBONY,* and *Heart & Soul,* as well as the book *Speaking of Success,* written by Stephen Covey and Jack Canfield.

A former board member of New York Academy of Art and YouthBridge-NY, Marsha remains committed to uplifting the next generation of changemakers and helping others move from stuck to unstoppable— one bold step at a time.

Rhonda Joy McLean is president and CEO of RJMLEADS LLC, a leadership consulting and career advancement company based in New York City. Her clientele include executives and institutions in the public, private, and academic sectors, as well as students of all ages. She is the former deputy general counsel of Time Inc., a global media company, where she managed one-third of the law department and provided legal counsel for nearly twenty years to over 200 clients, including *Time, Fortune, People, Sports Illustrated, Essence,* and other widely renowned brands. She has received awards throughout her career for her commitment to greater access to legal education for all and for supporting survivors of domestic violence.

ABOUT STOREHOUSE VOICES

Storehouse Voices celebrates culturally rich narratives that reflect the dynamic influence of communities across the globe. Our imprint is dedicated to amplifying underrepresented and overworthy voices in fiction and nonfiction, with a focus on accessible and engaging content that honors the past, disrupts the present, and imagines new futures.

Learn more about us at storehousevoices.com.